Anna Leonowens:
A Life Beyond
The King and I

Leslie Smith Dow

Pottersfield Press, Lawrencetown Beach
Nova Scotia
1991

Canadian Cataloguing in Publication Data

Smith Dow, Leslie
  Anna Leonowens
  ISBN 0-919001-69-6

1. Leonowens, Anna Harriet , 1831 - 1915 — Biography.
2. Authors, English — 19th century — Biography. I. Title.
   PR4883.L64Z85 1991 823'.8 C91-097612-0

Published with the support of the Nova Scotia Department of
Tourism and Culture and the Canada Council

Pottersfield Press
Lawrencetown Beach
RR 2, Porters Lake, Nova Scotia
Canada BOJ 2S0

The journey of a thousand miles begins with the first step.
Lao-tzu (604-531 B.C.)

This book is for Maude Alexandra and Margaret Dorothy, who always expected something like this would happen

And for Donald, who was certain

MIZPAH

Anna Harriet Leonowens as a young woman (circa 1861).

Anna Leonowens was rather small with a stately appearance, and everyone listened when she spoke in her beautiful voice. Piercing brown eyes looked out from a face whose complexion had been ruined by the climate of the Orient, and she wore her wavy grey hair parted in the middle, brushed upward and coiled into a pretzel on the top of her head, usually held in place with a silver comb.... She always wore a ring with an uncut emerald given to her by one of King Mongkut's wives, Lady Son Klin, and [a] tiger-claw brooch made from two of the tiger's claws set in fine engraved gold from the tiger which her husband had shot just before his death. After the heat of the Far East, she minded the cold in the big drafty rooms of the Halifax houses of the last century, and usually sat with a black shawl round her shoulders. Her daughter Avis kept asking: 'Are you warm enough, Mama?'[1]

Phyllis R. Blakeley, "Anna of Siam in Canada,"
The Atlantic Advocate, January, 1967.

Contents

Chronology

Glossary

Foreign words and expressions frequently used in this book (N.B.: These words are of Thai origin unless otherwise indicated):

mam (mem)	lady
mam cha	lady dear
wat	temple
Muang Thai	Kingdom of the free
chedi	Dome, usually covered in gold leaf, with a pointed spire, associated with Buddhist temples and found within the monastery grounds
chowfa	prince
maha	great and wise person kralahome prime minister
klong	canal
moonshee	teacher (Hindustani)
Pali	ancient Thai language used for Buddhist religious writings Sanskrit ancient Hindu language
farang	foreigner
p'hra	priest
ayah	children's nanny

Author's Note

Piecing together the life of Anna Leonowens has taken some detective work, some psychoanalysis, a good deal of reflection and sometimes, just plain intuition. There seemed to be something missing from the story of her life as I knew it, and I turned it over and over in my mind, searching for a hidden spring or some sort of code that would help me unravel the mystery of Anna. But there was none.

Gradually, though, after poring over her writing, her behaviour and the attitudes of her contemporaries, I began to see a clearer picture. Her past began to fill in, although I felt many times that I was painting by numbers, without the benefit of the numbers. Even after I had read everything I could get my hands on which referred to this most interesting woman, it seemed that somehow something wasn't quite right. Descriptions of her life were either too pat or too condemning. I found no less than four writers who had demolished her reputation and branded her a fake.

Such descriptions seemed to me eminently unfair. She was creative with the truth, to be sure, but not a fake. It is clear that she sought to keep certain elements of her background secret. Diligent research has served only to render the details of her life as she related it even more ambiguous. On the other hand, tantalizing fragments of another existence materialize when her own accounts are disregarded, and the pieces of what seems to have been a secret life begin to fall into place.

Depending on whom one chooses to believe, Anna Leonowens may have been among the most accomplished, fearless and adventurous of Victorian ladies, or a complete fake who covered up her ignoble origins by inventing and exaggerating at will, simply to sell copies of her books. Her story of a proper British governess confronting a monstrous Oriental monarch seems a trifle overdone. Even the most accommodating readers have had to make some effort to suspend their disbelief that a British governess could not only rise to become the right hand of the powerful and erudite King of Thailand, but to teach a man who spent 27 contemplative years as a Buddhist monk a thing or two about compassion. The truth, as with most things, lies in the boggy ground somewhere between the conflicting descriptions of Anna as a Victorian human rights crusader along the lines of Harriet Beecher Stowe, and Anna as a kind of benign Mata Hari of literature.

It was not until I made a chance visit to Fort Henry in Kingston, Ontario (which would have been in use around the time young Anna was growing up in India) that I was able to unlock some of the mystery surrounding Anna's early life. Anna grew up in an Anglo-Indian military family, whose domestic arrangements could only be described as squalid, a fact that hit home forcefully as I peppered the patient staff with questions about living conditions of army families in the colonies, including India. The stigma attached to being an "army rat," as such children were then called, was enormous, particularly for a girl. The chances of escaping a life following the drum were almost nil. Unless a particularly bright female could get on teaching at the regimental school, or nursing in the infirmary, she would almost certainly be forced, through sheer economic necessity, to marry a much older soldier at some time between her thirteenth and fifteenth birthdays.

Knowing these facts provided me with a motive for Anna's inventive vagueness about her past. It also partly explained her sudden appointment as royal governess. The seemingly inexperienced widow had likely been picked as a youngster to assist in the classroom. By the time she was 18, it would be reasonable to expect that she already had several years' teaching under her belt, in some tough classrooms. Drawing on her teaching experience, and fortified by her ambition and intelligence, Anna invented an appropriate background for her new life as a proper Victorian lady, much the same as famed explorer-journalist Henry Morton Stanley fabricated his. Her forceful personality and resilience helped her make the transition to a new life that would have been impossible for most other young women in her social situation. But that, surely, is beside the point. What is important is her gumption; she did what was necessary to achieve the sort of life on which she had set her sights.

There are no hard and fast answers about Anna's life. There are few details which can be verified beyond the shadow of a doubt and the sketchiness of many events in her life is partially due to the unfortunate habit of journalists (past and present) of simply copying what had previously been written about her. As my research progressed, I wondered why it was so impossible for her critics to praise in a woman the very qualities they applaud in male adventurers (particularly Stanley). Only a scant amount of independent research had actually been conducted into Anna's life, and consequently, errors in fact have mushroomed into widely-accepted legend.

The real Anna, possessed of such formidable talent and courage, was much more than an English governess at the Siamese court: she was a brilliant storyteller and lecturer, an accomplished journalist and celebrated author, an Oriental scholar and linguist, an adventurer and social activist. Unfortunately, by the time she died in 1915 in Montreal, Anna's adventures, and her marvellous talents, had been nearly forgotten.

In 1944, inspired by *The English Governess at the Siamese Court*, and *Siamese Harem Life*, Margaret Landon published her own rewritten and highly coloured version of Anna's life. It caused a sensation, comparable only to the publication of the original books in 1870 and 1872. By 1944, *Anna and the King of Siam* had been through 13 printings. *Reader's Digest* even came out with a condensed version. Landon's book was published in Sweden, Spain, and Thailand, and 12 countries in between, as well as in armed services and juvenile editions.

By 1951, Rodgers and Hammerstein had made Anna's Siamese excursion into a musical about "a splendid, wicked oriental court." Twentieth Century-Fox wasted no time in turning it into a movie. The tale was described gushingly on the back cover of the 1956 abridged pocket edition as a "charming true story" and as "one of the best-loved books and plays of our time." The late Yul Brynner, who played King Mongkut in both versions, "with scowling magnetism" according to a *Time* magazine review, became forever associated with the role. *Time's* critic also commented that, "This battle of sexes, collision of races and conflict of ideas, this spectacle of a king learning to govern from a governess, is sometimes touching, and far less insipid than the usual musicomedy romance." In 1989, the musical was revived with former ballet star Rudolph Nureyev in the lead, another icon playing icon.

But for all the attention they garnered, the books (beginning with Anna's own), the musical and the movie did not shed much light on the real Thailand, nor on the real Anna. The idea of a king "learning to govern from a governess" was absurd, and only partially because Anna's formidable adversary was hailed in his lifetime as Thailand's wisest ruler long before she arrived. The original book created an unfavourable stir in Thailand, where kings were and are treated with the reverence their status as divinities demands. Anna's own books still cannot be found in Thai bookstores, although accounts written by other adventurers, ranging back to a 17th-century emissary from the court of King Louis XIV of France are available. When *The English Governess* was first published, the Thai government allegedly tried to buy up the whole first printing with the intention of destroying it.

Anna's Adventures in the New World

Several years after Anna's death, a descendant of King Mongkut came close to the truth when he said Anna had spiced up the events in her book to help support her family. She did indeed know how to spin a tale. By the time she reached New York in the fall of 1867, after six years in the Siamese court, she had hatched a plan. The death of King Mongkut the following year cleared the way, in Anna's mind at least, for her to publicly divulge her story.

But public preoccupation with her experiences in Thailand was to overshadow all of her subsequent accomplishments. No one remembers that she went on to become an acclaimed lecturer and writer, as well as an effective and diligent social activist. Yet the story of her life has rarely been deemed worthy of more than a few columns in an occasional Canadian magazine or newspaper. Despite her aggressive philanthropy in Halifax and Montreal, the Anna Leonowens Gallery is the only institution in in Canada that bears her name.

The tale of *Anna and the King of Siam* is almost as well known around the globe as *Anne of Green Gables*. While Lucy Maud Montgomery's name is synonymous with her creation, the same cannot be said about Ann Harriet Emma Leonowens, who spent forty years of her life in Canada, all the while carefully guarding the truth about herself from everyone, even her own family. She was eloquent and intelligent enough not to betray to any curious journalist details that might lead to a thorough investigation of what was, in her own mind, a decidedly unsavoury background.

Even now, 76 years after her death, she remains the only person to ever knew the full story. Curiously, Anna either left no diary, or, tragically, it has long since been destroyed or lost.

Of necessity, what follows here is the product of my best abilities to reconstruct and interpret the life of Anna Leonowens with an open, but admittedly sympathetic, mind. Even so, I fear her finished portrait may still prove to be painted more in the style of the Impressionists than the Realists. As Don Akenson remarked so insightfully in his biography, *At Face Value: The Life and Times of Eliza McCormack/John White*, we can either go back to stark fact-grinding biographies (which in their selection and arrangement of facts are fictive, but in an unconscious and unexamined manner), or we can try to get inside our subject's mind — and in so doing accept the fact that biography, like many other forms of historical investigation, demands an energetic, self-conscious exercise of imagination.

There is no one view of the life, or lives, of this remarkable lady, only degrees of interpretation. Doubtless, further details confirming, denying or clarifying Anna's past will come to light in ensuing years. Perhaps further interest will even be sparked by the conclusions of this volume. My fondest hope is that through this book, Anna will once again be remembered.

Additional Notes

1. Throughout this volume I have tried to consistently use the names Thai and Thailand ("Muang Thai," the Thai name, means "kingdom of the free") in place of Siamese and Siam, except where reference has been made in this way in other texts. As Anna Leonowens explained in her book, *Siamese Harem Life*, these latter terms come from the Malaysian word "sagum," meaning "the brown race," considered derogatory by Thais.

2. Anna Leonowens was born Ann Harriet Emma Edwards yet she gave her name as Anna Harriet Crawford. Her husband's name was Thomas Leon Owens, and she referred to him as Leon. It would appear Anna did not use the surname Leonowens until after her husband's death, perhaps as a way of making herself seem more exotic and less easily traceable. Essentially, I have used the name Leon Owens for early references to Anna's husband, and the name Leonowens for the period of her life beginning with her widowhood.

Acknowledgements

I am indebted to many people for their assistance, support and faith, most particularly my late mother and grandmother (each of whom undertook the burden of my early education in true Anna Leonowens style), and my husband, Donald Dow, who knew I could do this before I did.

The financial assistance of the Canada Council was crucial to the completion of this project, and the encouragement and support of the Explorations staff was gratefully received.

Thanks are owed Joan Fairlie, Anna's great-granddaughter; Dr. Thomas Fyshe, her great-grandson; Jonathan Fyshe, her great-great-grandson, for telling me all they knew about their ancestor, and to my friend P'hra Maha Wallop Suswad of Wat Parinayok, Bangkok, for his hands-on demonstrations of the practical applications of Theravada Buddhism, as well as interesting conversations about Anna and King Mongkut.

Thanks to Maud Rosinski, who brought Victorian Halifax alive for me (and to Marjory Whitelaw for leading me to her); to Prof. Harold Pearse of NSCAD for trusting me to give credit where credit is due for his painstakingly-retrieved original research; to the inventor of Interlibrary Loan; to the staff at the Public Archives of Nova Scotia, especially Lois Kernaghan, Garry Shutlak and Margaret Campbell, for their diligence; the interpretive guides at Fort Henry in Kingston, Ontario, for answering my myriad questions on army life; staff at the McGill University Archives and the rare book department; and British researcher J. D. Parry for unearthing valuable details from British parish registers and the records of the East India Company.

Heartfelt thanks to Claire McIlveen and Ed Head for their for accommodations while I was in Halifax (three times), and for taking me to the beach when I needed it; to Dave Morefield (ditto); to Sandra Clarke for her patience and understanding; and finally, to Lesley Choyce, for the great enthusiasm with which he took this leap of faith.

Grateful acknowledgement is herewith made for permission to use the following material: The Halifax Herald Ltd. for allowing me to quote freely from *The Evening Chronicle, The Acadian Recorder, The Mercury, The Halifax Herald, The Evening Mail, The Morning Herald, The Morning Chronicle* and *The Mail-Star*; the Rodgers and Hammerstein Organization for use of the title, "The King and I;" permission granted by the Bank of Nova Scotia

Archives for the Fyshe Letterbook and *The Scotiabank Story* by Joseph Schull and Douglas J. Gibson, MacMillan of Canada (Toronto, 1982); Bechert, Heinz and Richard Gombrich, eds. *The World of Buddhism*, Facts on File Publications (New York, 1984); Blakeley, Phyllis R. "Anna of Siam in Canada" in *The Atlantic Advocate*, Jan. 1967, vol. 57, no. 4, pp. 41-45; the Public Archives of Nova Scotia for use of the Blakeley Collection; minute and record books of the Victoria School of Art and Design, the Halifax Local Council of Women and the Halifax Ladies College, as well as photographs of Anna Leonowens, Thomas Fyshe, Sr. and Thomas Fyshe, Jr. and historic locations in Halifax; Buckler, William E., ed. *Prose of the Victorian Period*, Houghton Mifflin Co. (Boston, 1958); Burns, H. D. "Thomas Fyshe, 1845-1911" in *Canadian Banker*, Autumn, 1951; Collard, Edgar Andrew, "When Anna came to Canada," in *The Montreal Gazette*, Jan. 27, 1979; *The Private Capital* by Sandra Gwynn (used by permission of Mc-Clelland & Stewart, Toronto); Jumsai, M. L. Manich, *King Mongkut and Sir John Bowring*, Chalermnit (Bangkok, 1970); Keay, Julia, *With Passport and Parasol: The adventures of seven Victorian ladies*, BBC Books (London, 1989); Landon, Margaret, *Anna and the King of Siam*, Pocket Books of Canada Ltd., Cardinal abridged ed. (Montreal, 1956); MacNaughton, John. "Mrs. Leonowens," orig. published *The University Magazine*, McGill University, 1915; rpt. *Essays and Addresses*, no. 19, pp. 286-311 (permission granted by McGill University Archives); *New York Times*, Jan. 24-Feb. 10, 1888; *Time* magazine, "New Musical in Manhattan," Apr. 9, 1951; Akenson, Don, *At Face Value: The Life and Times of Eliza Mc-Cormack/John White*, McGill-Queen's University Press, Montreal & Kingston, 1990; Abrams, Donaldson, Smith et al, eds., *Rudyard Kipling's Verse, Definitive Edition*, "The Ladies," Bantam Doubleday Dell Publishing Group Inc.; Beecher Stowe, Harriet, *Uncle Tom's Cabin*, Bantam Doubleday Dell Publishing Group Inc. and *Saturday Night* magazine. Material reprinted with permission of Macmillan Publishing Company from *Thailand: The New Siam* by Virginia Thompson, Copyright 1941 by International Secretariat, Institute of Pacific Relations, renewed © 1968 by Mrs. Virginia Adloff.

Prologue

The Secret Life of Anna
1831-1861

The woman the world would come to know as Mrs. Anna Harriet Leonowens was brought into the world on a tiny cot at the back of a stifling hot East India Company barracks on November 6, 1831 in Ahmednugger, India.[1] It was no accident that this squalid corner was where the second daughter of Thomas and Mary Anne Edwards made her first frown: it was home.

Anna never admitted to her humble origins. She always maintained her father was an officer, despite the absence of any supporting documents to prove her claim. In fact, baptismal and marriage records show her father and stepfather were both enlisted men, who had signed on for an indefinite term in the private army maintained by the East India Company. Such service normally lasted 21 years, if the soldier survived. Many recruits succumbed, victims of poor living conditions and low morale in the best of times, or struck down by more tangible enemies in times of war.

Anna was mostly silent about her origins, only hinting at upper-class existence marred from time to time by tragedy. It was well she resisted the temptation to invent too much, for her depiction of herself as "a young girl fresh from school"[2] was the approach which she rightly calculated would win her the greatest sympathy. In her later incarnation as an author, it was an approach which also won her many fans. In her autobiographical third book, *Life and Travel in India*, Anna recounted how she marvelled, as her boat steamed into the harbour, at the wonders of Bombay. She noted she later spent one or two years in Puna with her family, where her stepfather was "connected with the engineer or public works department at the military station...."[3] This claim, however, is not borne out by any military records. Anna avoided stating outright the claim later made by Margaret Landon in *Anna and the King of Siam* that she was born and

1

educated in Carnaervon, Wales, preferring to let her readers come to their own conclusions.

It seems more plausible to assume her childhood was spent in the fecund confines of an Indian barracks. Only a screen divided the family's cramped back corner from the raucous noises of upwards of two dozen men eating, drinking, gambling, undressing and sleeping.[4] Little Anna (baptized Ann Harriet Emma Edwards) and her elder sister, Eliza Julia (born on April 26, 1830) would have had a good view of the incessant activity from their pallets underneath their parents' cots.[5]

Later in life, Anna refused to talk about her stepfather, Patrick Donohoe, and could provide few details about her natural father, Thomas Edwards. What she did reveal she had made up. Military records show Thomas Edwards, a brown-haired, grey-eyed former cabinetmaker from Middlesex, England, joined an East India Company infantry regiment on April 6, 1824. After three years of good conduct and hard work, he was granted leave to marry. Four years later (and having survived seven years of service in India) he had risen to the rank of sergeant. But life in the Orient was hot and hard. In August or September of 1831, Thomas Edwards died.

His death left Anna's mother, Mary Anne Glasscott Edwards, in dire straits. For one thing, she was six months' pregnant. For another thing, she, Eliza, and her unborn child (Anna) would be stricken off the strength in another six months. And that would mean no more rations, even if they were only boiled beef and hard bread, and no more free accommodation inside the garrison. The army could make arrangements for certain families to receive passage to England, but it was unlikely to transport Mary Anne, who had been born in India and never even seen that green and pleasant land.

Although it was not unheard of for able-bodied army widows to receive marriage proposals even before their husband's funeral service had ended, Mary Anne held out for the full six months before resigning herself to the inevitable. On January 9, 1832, she married Patrick Donohoe, just three months after Anna was born. Once again, the family set up housekeeping in the back corner of the stifling barracks. Life had scarcely changed.

Born in Bengal, India to Anne Glasscott and her husband, John, an artillery gunner, Mary Anne was no stranger to the privations of army life. There is no record of the marriage of Anne and John Glasscott, but soldiers routinely took common-law wives for the duration of their postings despite strict punishments meted out for contravening army regulations.[6] Only six out of every 100 enlisted men were allowed to marry[7], although officers obtained the required permission more frequently. While legally married soldiers received an extra half ration for their wives, and a quarter ration for each of their children, soldiers with common-law wives received nothing.

Soldiers' wives had to be more than equal to the tough lives they had chosen. They were encouraged to supplement their husbands' meager wages by doing the regiment's wash, and a bride was often chosen for her hardiness as much as anything else. The soldiers respected and feared their female camp followers, who fought and won their own battles, with tongues or fists.

It was a way of life the children learned quickly, as they paraded around in their fathers' hand-me-down uniforms and their mothers' old dresses. But the children were kept busy, and were well-educated by the standards of the time. Six days a week they attended school. On the seventh day, they went to church, and in between times, they helped with chores.

Each morning, as soon as they were old enough, girls helped their mothers scrub out their sleeping area and air their mattresses. After breakfast, they helped clean the garrison's privies before heading to the school room. Attendance was compulsory, and fathers were liable for punishment if their children were truant. For garrison children, learning the arts of reading, writing and arithmetic began at age four.

Anna would have received her early education in a garrison school, considered so superior to private local schools that even officers sent their children. Although her early education would have consisted of large doses of British history, literature, and culture, Anna's real enthusiasm was piqued by her study of India's languages and literature, its religions and its history.

But it scarcely mattered what her interests were. Like the other garrison children, Anna's schooling officially ended at age 15. While boys were expected to enlist or seek their fortunes elsewhere, the options for girls were sharply reduced. Teaching, nursing or marriage were the only respectable routes open to them. Patrick Donohoe seems to have decided upon the latter

3

course of action for his stepdaughters, and at age 14, sister Eliza married 38-year-old Sergeant-Major James Millard on April 24, 1845. The ceremony came just in time, for Eliza celebrated her fifteenth birthday two days later, and would not have been entitled to live within the garrison much longer.

Anna, a witness at the wedding, must have decided there and then she must escape her sister's fate. She had little taste for a marriage of convenience, but unless she secured herself a position as assistant monitor or even assistant schoolmistress, her only other options would be to serve as an army nurse in some disease-infested hospital, or to fend for herself. Hiring out as servants was a popular avenue of escape, but for girls like Eliza and Anna, it would have been impossible. Their upbringing in an army barracks was widely considered to be fundamentally immoral, and no society woman would knowingly darken her door with that sort of girl.

It was just as well. Anna's inherent cleverness, aptitude for teaching, and no-nonsense personality would have certainly qualified her to stay on in the classroom. She may well have been taken on as an assistant schoolmistress, and fortuitously been able to avoid marriage for the time being. It is entirely likely that she first attracted the attention of Reverend George Percy Badger in a garrison school.

As regimental chaplain of the East India Company in Puna[8] (where Anna's family had been transferred), he was required to inspect and supervise the school and the sergeant schoolmaster. It would have been logical and practical for Anna's stepfather to urge their union. Anna always maintained he had tried to marry her to a rich merchant twice her age, and her refusal caused a rift within the family which never healed. (In fact, the 30-year-old minister would have been exactly twice Anna's age.)

When it came time for Reverend Badger, a scholarly man with a lively interest in all things Oriental, to go on an extended leave to the Middle East and Egypt, Anna went along. She swore she made the trip with Reverend Badger and his wife, but it is possible Anna posed as his wife in order to avoid a scandal.

But the headstrong Anna had already met her man: the young, dynamic Thomas Leon Owens, a clerk in the military pay office, to whom she had become engaged before her trip. Despite her wholehearted devotion to her studies of Egyptian culture, art and architecture (she also learned Persian and Arabic), her feelings for Reverend Badger did not change while they were away. Marriage records show that on Christmas Day, 1849, Harriet Edwards and Thomas Leon Owens wed. Notably, Reverend Badger did not officiate! The family's reaction could hardly have been as bad as she later intimated, for Patrick Donohoe attended, as did Eliza and her husband, John Donohoe and N. F. Glasscott. The name of Anna's mother, Mary Anne, was not on the register, perhaps an indication that her mother, not her stepfather, was the parent who was more upset about the marriage.

The couple returned to Bombay, where their first child, a daughter named Selena Louisa, was born December 10, 1850. Selena died at the age of 17 months, and was buried May 24, 1852 at Colaba, on the southern end of Bombay Island.

During the next 10 years, the family apparently did a good deal of travelling, but it is not clear in what capacity. Thomas was evidently made a Brevet-Major at some point, an honorary military title. Anna said they lived in England and Australia. While in Australia, she apparently gave birth to a second child, who later died. Two more children were born, Avis Annie Connybeare on October 25, 1854, and Louis Thomas Gunnis on October 25, 1855, supposedly in London, England.[9] Eventually, the family made its way to Southeast Asia. One theory puts Leon as a hotel keeper in Penang, Malaysia, with Anna no doubt his trusty, slightly formidable assistant. But in 1858 or 1859, Leon suddenly died, of either a heart attack or heat stroke.[10]

Like her mother 27 years before, Anna unexpectedly found herself in the precarious position of having two small children to raise, and nothing whatever to sustain them. Although her circumstances were only slightly better than her mother's, she appears to have ruled out remarriage entirely, despite several attractive proposals. Marriage may have made her life easier in the short term but it would close forever the door to freedom she saw opening before her.

It is quite possible she may have landed a position as an assistant schoolmistress at the British garrison in Singapore. Her claim to have opened a school for officers' children is less likely, since the usual practice was for such children to either be sent home to a British boarding school, or to attend the regimental school, where standards of education were far and away better than anything commonly available publicly or privately. It is not certain what Anna did to earn a living during the three years

5

following her husband's death, but it can be assumed she taught in some kind of school. Whatever her position, her salary would have been meagre.

But Anna wanted more. In 1862, she got what she wanted. It was the job of a lifetime.

Endnotes

1. British researcher J. D. Parry's search of East India Company records show Anna was baptised Dec. 6, 1831 in Ahmednugger. The town has a large fort, built in 1550, where former Indian Prime Minister Jawaharlal Nehru was once imprisoned by the British.

2. Leonowens, Anna. *Life and Travel in India*, Porter and Coates (Philadelphia, 1884), p. 7.

3. Leonowens, Anna. *Life and Travel in India*, *op.cit.* p. 39

4. Another enlisted man's family occupied the other back corner of the barracks.

5. Anna would not have enjoyed the comforts of what passed for a real bed until she left the garrison (normally around age 15). Army children were not issued cots, nor was there any extra space in which to put one. Boys were sometimes allowed to sleep in the cots of absent soldiers, but never girls.

6. Researcher J. D. Parry failed to turn up a marriage record.

7. This number varied slightly from regiment to regiment.

8. In 1817, Puna became the British capital of the Southern Maharashtra region during the monsoon season.

9. Researcher J. D. Parry could find no record of their births in Britain.

10. Anna maintained her husband died in her arms of heatstroke brought on by a vigorous tiger hunt in Singapore.

A seventeenth-century map of Old Siam, drawn for Monsieur
le Chevalier de Chaumont, Ambassador to Siam.

Chapter One

An English Governess at the Siamese Court

> And now began the era of Mrs. Leonowens' life which
> has had no parallel in modern times, and has made the
> recital of its events as "interesting as a story from the
> Arabian Nights."[1]

Right up until she stepped off the steamer *Chao Phya*, named for
the Chao Phya Menam river that winds through Bangkok, Anna
had been warned by friends and strangers alike not to become
King Mongkut's English governess. She ignored them. She
needed a job, and with characteristic aplomb she had accepted.

Had she been able to look in a mirror at that moment, Anna
Leonowens would have seen a darkly handsome woman whose
eyes exuded passion and self-possession. She was neither short
nor tall, and, in her youth her dark, curly hair cascaded over her
shoulders. She was the sort of woman at whom passersby would
turn to stare, and whose intense personality was revealed in a
gaze so direct and searching that it sometimes made people feel
uncomfortable.

But Anna didn't have much time for glass-gazing; good
looks and charisma could only make up for so much of what she
felt was lacking in her life. Her plans, like her manner, were bold.

Anna stood on deck as the steamer drew into port. The heavy
Bangkok air was so thick she felt it clogging her throat as she took
a breath. It was still only March, the Ides of March, to be exact, in
the year 1862, and the hot season had not yet prostrated the city.
When travelling, Anna much preferred the euphoria of arrival to
the actual journey. Being cooped up in a tiny cabin eating
monotonous shipboard meals each day was hardly her idea of
adventure, but she relished the moment of arrival and the atten-
dant excitement of setting foot on new shores. But she had never
been to Bangkok before, and she found her anticipation at ending
a long sea voyage had been tempered by more than a little
apprehension. No matter how brave a face she put on in public,
she had to quietly admit to herself that she was a little nervous
about meeting the temperamental monarch she had heard so
much about.

As soon as the ship was moored fast, the deck swarmed with stevedores. For the first time in her life, Anna hesitated. She drew Louis closer to her. Bessy, the family's protective Newfoundland dog, sensed her unease and sat down at their feet. Moonshee, her Persian tutor, and Beebe, his wife, and ayah to Louis, simply looked at her, inured to whatever might be in store for them in this foreign country, and waited patiently to disembark.

She wondered if she had made the right decision in bringing her precocious six-year-old son Louis with her to this strange new land. She was his sole protector now that her dear Leon was dead. Perhaps she should have sent him to boarding school in Britain with Avis, who had put on such a brave face. Anna was certainly relieved Avis was not with her, for the sensitive and intuitive seven-year-old would have instantly perceived her mother's reluctance, and would have been alarmed. It would be six months before she would even receive word that her little girl had arrived safely! But there could be no going back, for there was nothing to go back to.

Anna continued to stand at the rail, waiting for some sort of sign that she should proceed into this new land. No one at all seemed to care that she had come. All manner of boats plied their way to and fro, loaded to the gunwales with people or provisions or both. Except for the flurry of activity back and forth across the river, Anna was tempted to think, by peering at the banks of the Chao Phya Menam (whose name meant *great mother river*) that there was no city at all nearby. Everywhere, jostling for space in lush confusion, were banana trees, palm trees and flowering bushes whose exuberance defied description. Young children, sleek as muskrats, dove and cavorted in the river as their grandfathers and grandmothers slept in the doorways of dark teak houses perched on stilts out of reach of the highest waters. Wearing distinctive straw hats, women perched atop dugout canoes filled with vegetables, meats or even flowers plied the small canals between the dwellings.

Anna scanned the riverbank and the quay, not for a famliar face, for she knew no one in Bangkok, but simply for a helpful one. Yet it seemed no representative from the royal household was on hand to meet her, and she had no idea how to get to the palace herself. She began to think that the whole adventure might have been a horrible mistake. Perhaps she should have listened to the warnings given so freely by friends and strangers.

She could have accepted the proposal of marriage made by the gracious and refined Dr. Francis Cobb, but at the time, her grief over Leon's death had been too fresh. There was still time for her to give in to the attentions of Captain Orton, who was certainly handsome. But the thought of a lifetime spent swaying over the ocean, eating salted meat and listening to the clumsy but ardent expression of his typically British prejudices was just too much. She was better off dancing with an entirely new devil, even if she wasn't quite sure how she would recognize him.

While she stood dithering on deck, Anna's thoughts turned to the circumstances of her unusual employment. It had all begun in a surprisingly straightforward way. The king had written to his consul in Singapore, Tan Kim Ching, about the possibility of procuring an English governess to teach his wives and children. The matter had also come to the attention of the manager of the Borneo Company's Singapore branch, William Adamson.

Without hesitation, Mr. Adamson, having been previously stationed in Bangkok and still in regular correspondence with the Siamese king, recommended Anna for the job. Mr. Tan, upon meeting her, also gave his wholehearted endorsement. Both men instantly perceived her innate capability, her obvious intelligence, and her quiet confidence. Mr. Adamson could attest to the way she easily captured and held her pupils' imaginations and interests with her exotic stories, which always ended with a moral or puzzle. He sent his own children to the garrison school where she taught, and they were forever coming home breathless to relate a new story told to them by Mrs. Leonowens. Her stories, were often about tolerance and self-improvement, although she deliberately refrained from pointed religious references. Through his long association with the Siamese monarch, Mr. Adamson knew it was exactly the sort of thing Maha Mongkut was sure to approve of!

He was right. Not long after the interview, Mr. Adamson was able to report to an anxious Anna that he thought things were proceeding very favourably indeed. A little later, he showed her a letter the king had sent him in Feb. 27, 1862, which confirmed his opinion. But when she read over the letter, the new governess found she was hardly uppermost in the king's thoughts. First and foremost, he seemed concerned about procuring some cannons just like those which had belonged to

Sir James Brooke, the recently retired white rajah of nearby Sarawak. It was not until page two of the letter that he got around to negotiating the terms of Anna's employment, and she had to admit, he was a tough customer.

Shrewdly, he managed to reduce her promised salary by one-third before she even arrived, and insisted that she live nowhere near the American missionaries (as originally planned) whose influence upon her he dreaded:

> ...we have learnt that the said Lady agree to receive an only salary of $100 per month & accept to live in this palace or nearest place hereof, I am very glad to have her be our school mistress if the said information be true. I can give her a brick house in nearest vicinity of this palace if she would desire to live with her husband or mail (male) servant .....[2]

If the king was careful to set out his exact expectations of her conduct, it was because he had learned from painful past experience what to expect from aspiring English-speaking royal educators:

> ...it is not pleasant to us if the school mistress much morely endeavour to convert the scholars to Christianity than teaching language literature &c. like the American Missionaries here, because our proposed expense is for knowledge of the important language & literature which will be useful for affairs of country not for the religion which is yet disbelieved by Siamses [sic] scholars in general.[3]

Soon after Anna's acceptance of the offer, the king reconfirmed his expectations that

> in doing your education on us and on our children (whom English call inhabitants of benighted land) you will do your best endeavour for knowledge of English language, science and literature, and not for conversion to Christianity.[4]

The king had every reason to be cautious. He did not relish any further religious rows with the American missionaries, who were a prickly group if ever there was one.

In truth, pickings in the governess department were rather slim. Not many English women were willing to leave the relative safety of the British colony for what was perceived as the wild and heathen wilderness of Siam. Anna could still hear the proper old matrons clucking their tongues and shaking their heads at her in dismay. That Anna would consent to do so without the protective influence of a husband, and that she would even consider bringing up her young son in that den of iniquity was so far beyond the bounds of propriety that it was scarcely comprehensible. More than one woman intimated she would likely wind up as part of that infernal heathen's harem.

Anna had no time for their sort of nonsense. Those women, she reasoned, only pretended to be perfectly content with their lives, and took comfort in the misbegotten belief that to be British was to be the best. Anna didn't have much faith in their smug belief of their own superiority; she had always lived on the boundaries of that society without ever being completely accepted into it. Despite herself, she yearned to be a part of that world which revolted her with its snobbery and rejection of anything that was not British. She hated the colonizers attempts to convert the Hindus and the Buddhists to Christianity and mourned the gradual disintegration of indigenous culture in the onslaught of imported British culture.

Those smug matrons would never set foot in a Hindu temple or pray at a Buddhist shrine; they knew no languages but the Queen's English and resisted learning any but the few words useful for ordering their servants about. They were revolted by the idea of harems, but had no conception of what life could be like for any woman who was not privileged enough to be so honoured by her lord. Anna hated the lack of liberty and justice of those women who lived within the harem walls, yet had been familiar with the practice since early childhood.

What Anna really detested was being treated as a perpetual outsider. She knew full well she was not welcome at the club that comprised virtually all of British middle and upper class society. But it was not her fault her father and stepfather had never received decent educations, or that the thick accents of their soldiers' tongues were evident in their daughter's unclipped accent. It was not her fault (indeed, she hardly thought it a fault at all) that her mother's skin was thought to be just a shade too dark to be thoroughly British, or that she found British history dull and sanctimonious. She could read Latin fluently, but she preferred Persian. Yet intelligence and resourcefulness were not prerequisites for admission to the social strata she sought to occupy. In fact, short of being re-born as someone else, there was nothing she could do to erase the traces of her upbringing in a certain squalid little Indian garrison town, where British soldiers and their families spent the eternities of their days gambling, drinking and fighting. Or was there?

Despite the continual family quibbles and quarrels, and the occasional all-out battle, Anna had loved her childhood days in India. In Ahmednugger, her birthplace, she had rambled about the backstreets, an urchin like all the rest, prattling on in Hindustani or English or the strange Guzerati tongue her mother had taught her, or a combination of all three. She loved the religious processions of the Muslims, the ceremonies of the Sikhs and the funerals of the Hindus. She knew the rituals of the Brahmins and the tricks of the street performers. She discovered a deep and abiding interest in other cultures that was to stay with her for the rest of her life, and which would prove her greatest, if least recognized, gift.

Just then, Anna's shipboard reverie was shattered by a terrific ruckus. She was stunned to see the entire crew, with the exception of the vessel's master, Captain Orton, and her own two servants, fall on their faces. Two exquisite dragon-shaped boats, propelled by dozens of muscular rowers, had shot out quickly from shore, reaching the ship in a matter of moments. Now, climbing out of the magnificent crafts and onto the deck of the ship was a regal party.

"The kralahome, Ma'am," Captain Orton whispered in her ear. Seconds later, his entourage squatted like frogs in front of their lord, who alone remained standing. It was obvious this kralahome was a man of great power; his penetrating gaze alone was enough to convince Anna of that fact. She assumed the men grovelling at his feet were slaves; in fact, anyone of lower rank (in this case anyone but the king) was obliged to lay prostrate before the prime minister. Europeans were no longer required to perform the difficult and frog-like prostration.

Anna tried to look the prime minister in the face, but she found her eyes were glued instead to his muscular chest. A red silk skirt hung gracefully down to his ankles — and that was all. Of course, bare-chested men were nothing new to her; she had seen many Oriental labourers who were too poor to even possess a shirt. She was embarassed, though, at seeing a man of such power standing before her in such a posture, a look of passionate hauteur on his face. She felt her own face grow red, and she covered her embarrassment with anger. Instead of the deep curtsy that proper English etiquette would have demanded at her introduction to the number two man in the kingdom Anna gave only a slight nod of her head. To behave so before the most influential man in the kingdom was a serious gaffe, but she didn't care.

Things quickly went from bad to worse as the prime minister pelted the new governess with questions. No, she had no friends in Bangkok. No, she did not know what she would do or where she would sleep tonight. "I am a stranger here," she said, her voice as cold as it could be, "but I understand from His Majesty's letter that a residence would be provided for me on my arrival. And he has been informed that we were to arrive at this time."[5]

The tired, embarrassed and now irritated Anna knew her responses would be seen as bordering on the belligerent, but she thought it best to put up a strong front from the beginning. To allow herself to be perceived as weak and vacillating was the worst mistake she could make. She knew the simple fact that she was a woman would be enough reason for many people to dismiss her outright. Anna was not one to play the part of the helpless female, even if such behaviour might be more likely to help her accomplish her aims.

The prime minister, for his part, could hardly believe what he was hearing. Was this strange English woman piqued because she had not been immediately swept up and conducted to her very own house? Or was she perhaps upset because only he, the prime minister, had met her, and not the king himself? It was really too much. He didn't like her one bit, but good manners prevented him from saying so. "His Majesty cannot remember everything!" he retorted. "You can go wherever you like!"[6] And with that, he strode back to his boat, leaving the exasperated Anna and her beleaguered household on deck. In spite of herself, she had lost round one, and she knew it. Now, for all she knew, they would have to spend a sleepless night on deck, at the mercy of whomever might happen along. Worse still, she might have to fight off the amorous advances of Captain Orton.

Had Anna remembered to pack her sense of humour in her steamer trunk, she might have realized that what happened next was all part of the kralahome's inspired rebuke. After his abrupt departure, the prime minister called at the palace of the very popular Prince Wongsa, where the city's foreign residents had gathered with many of the nobles to watch some amateur theatrics. The uppity governess was left waiting for an hour before the kralahome sent the harbour master, Captain John Bush, out to the steamer to rescue Anna and her entourage. All were eventually stowed in Capt. Bush's launch, and they set off up the broadly curving Menam River to the Prince's home, known as The Palace to the Front because of its strategic location.

Despite her bad humour, Anna couldn't help but gape as they passed temple after temple, the intricate roof tiles and brilliant decorations flashing gold, green, blue and red in the late afternoon sun. Stylized dragons stood guard along the eaves trimmed in carved teak which resembled lace more than wood. Capt. Bush duly reeled off their names to her: Wat Po, Wat Rakang and Wat Pathum Kongka. He was especially careful to point out the various fairy-tale constructions glinting behind the crenellated walls of the Grand Palace, home of her new employer, and soon to be her own place of work. What she would discover behind its walls, Anna hadn't the slightest idea.

When the sorry group straggled into the palace, the prime minister could not contain his laughter. The new teacher, who was quite willing to accept the fact that she had been abandoned to her fate, had a look on her face that was sour enough to turn milk. She had been put in her place by a master, and didn't even know it. Fortunately, her first day in Bangkok was soon over.

The night was spent at the home of Captain Bush. Although she was thankful for his hospitality, she would soon find her second day in the "kingdom of the free" had dawned no more auspiciously than the first.

The kralahome sent for Anna early in the morning; their second meeting proved no more amicable. Anna, still tired and testy from the events of the night before, was on the defensive from the beginning. She lashed out when he asked her innocently enough how long her husband had been dead. Yet Anna was familiar with the Oriental custom of asking direct personal questions at the beginning of a conversation. Privately, she wondered whether the prime minister thought she was somehow less qualified, or more vulnerable, or even less of a person because she did not have a husband. Or was it true what the Singapore matrons had said about her winding up in a harem?

Anxious to settle herself and her son in their own accommodations, Anna's patience was at an end. She vented her frustrations on the kralahome's interpreter. Committing another gaffe, she mistook him for a servant:

Tell your master that his rights do not extend to the point of prying into my domestic concerns. His business with me is in my capacity of governess only. On other subjects I decline conversation.[9]

The prime minister, who spoke fluent English, took little notice of this strange new employee's puzzling brashness. To her demand for privacy, he merely replied, "As you wish." She was soon settled in private apartments within the kralahome's harem. But privacy remained elusive, for Anna soon found herself deluged with questions by the prime minister's extremely curious wives. It was several days before she got any peace.

Despite her efforts to put up a strong front, Anna had already succeeded in creating two enemies: the first two Thais she met took an instant dislike to her. Without knowing it, she had gravely insulted the interpreter who was not only an aristocrat but the half-brother of the kralahome, and a trusted aide. Throughout her stay, he made her life difficult in ways she had not imagined possible.

Yet Anna might be forgiven her inability to separate servants from nobles. Only native-born Thais could possibly be expected to figure out the complex system, about which it was said no two people shared the same rank. It took some time for Anna to realize that prostration, that strange Thai custom which required passersby to grovel in the dirt whenever they encountered someone of higher rank, did not indicate the subservience of slave to master, but was a mark of respect performed by people of all ranks.[9]

Anna was beginning to believe the ominous day of her arrival, the Ides of March, might cast a pall over her entire stay. And she may have been right, for she couldn't seem to keep herself, or her retinue, out of trouble. It was, after all, a perplexing country of highly complex etiquette and labrynthine manoeuverings, where it seemed every one of her tentative forays turned into a blunder.

Although she had been in the country less than forty-eight hours, she soon found herself embroiled in a matter of life and death. Her Persian teacher, Moonshee, had somehow wandered into the kralahome's harem. It was an offence punishable by immediate execution, for the only man permitted behind the harem's walls was its owner, as the old tutor well knew. By the time his wife had fetched Anna, he was on his knees and his mumbled prayers were tumbling down over his white beard. Instead of bemoaning his tragic accident, Moonshee was preparing himself to meet his fate.

Anna had waded into the fray without a thought for her own safety or any concern that she might lose her job, even when it became obvious Moonshee would simply be flogged as punishment for his blunder. Anna had seen the hideous punishments inflicted on scores of British soldiers during her lifetime; her own stepfather's back frequently bore bloody stripes from the cat o'nine tails. That someone under own protection should be so treated was unthinkable.[10] It was only later that she admitted to herself she had been foolhardy in threatening to call the British consul if the pundit was harmed. She had no idea if the consul would support her or not. She hadn't even called on him yet, another serious breach of etiquette.

When the kralahome appeared, Anna heaved a sign of relief in spite of herself. Although all of their meetings had so far been confrontational, she felt in her heart that he was a fair man. Her instincts were right: he instantly freed the grateful Moonshee. After the episode, Anna was left alone. Too alone.

Nearly six weeks passed. Anna hadn't even met her employer, let alone received any indication when school would start. While she waited, she roamed about Bangkok, learning its narrow waterways by heart, and learning to adjust to its torrid humidity. She began to envy the Thai women their boyish brush-cuts and unisex baggy pants. Truly, her hoopskirt was not the easiest outfit in which to climb in and out of a tippy dugout canoe, nor were her long curls and heavy sun bonnet at all comfortable in this weather. Her garments would be soaking wet within minutes of stepping out of the gates of the kralahome's palace. All her years in the Orient had not prepared her for this. Still, she had to keep Louis and herself busy while she waited for the king to summon her, and she felt it prudent to learn as much as she could about her new surroundings.

Anna delved into the country's history with the assistance of her new friends, the American missionaries. With the help of an elderly tutor, she began studying the Thai language. But her studies could not relieve her growing anxiety and restlessness. She was eager to tackle her teaching duties, but dared not suggest that the time was ripe for her to begin.

Finally, the long-awaited day of her audience with His Majesty the King was at hand. Anna put on the lavender dress she had worn the day of her arrival in Bangkok. After a reasonably successful attempt to tame Louis's rebellious hair, it was time to go. Taking him firmly by the hand, she stepped resolutely out of the kralahome's palace. Captain Bush was waiting for her; it was he who would present her at court.

It was only a short boat ride across the Great Mother River to the pier outside the Grand Palace. Anna had already had plenty of time to gape in wonderment at the magnificent gold and bejewelled rooftops of the palace complex, but now the huge gates were opened to admit the trio. Inside, Anna saw sights which exceeded her wildest imaginings. Behind the high walls were ornate gardens, statues of huge garuda birds, giant dancing demons and pouncing lion dogs, the huge gold-encrusted domes of the temple chedis, and the fantastic temple roofs with their multiple tiers and rainbow hues. Boldly drawn murals depicted the life of Buddha and told fantastic tales from Thai mythology. An awesome display of wealth and power was manifested in the art around her, and Anna couldn't help but feel intimidated.

But there was more waiting in store for Anna. She fidgeted as she waited behind one of the huge, decorated pillars in the king's vast audience hall, irritated at the prospect of spending yet another day awaiting the summons of the Lord of Life. Poor Louis was beginning to melt under the weight of his one good jacket, which was unfortunately made of tweed.

Instead of waiting quietly for the king to come to her, as a prudent throng of noblemen was already doing, Anna insisted that the embarrassed Captain Bush present her straight away.[10] He remonstrated with her, but she was firm. Taking a deep breath, Captain Bush escorted Anna and Louis up the steps to the lavish audience hall.

Within seconds, the king had spied his unsummoned guests. "Who? Who? Who?" he yelled.

Anna's heart sunk at the sight of the wizened, fierce-looking old man in baggy trousers stomping quickly towards the trio. He gazed at Anna intently and she stood in silence, hoping she was not outwardly trembling. She had no idea what would happen next. Then, to her great relief, the king stuck out his hand, in the English manner, for her to shake. So flustered was she that she returned no curtsy, and the thought of prostrating herself before him never entered her mind.

King Mongkut appeared not to have noticed her poor etiquette, and instead of relegating her to the end of the queue of supplicants, began asking her, in rapid-fire bursts, a series of personal questions. Although such questions were considered polite conversation in that country, Anna had more than a sneaking suspicion her answers would be the test of her mettle, and, possibly, her suitability for her new position.

"How old shall you be?" he asked bluntly.

Anna hesitated. There was precious little she could say that would give her an edge over the king's authority, but she knew the aged were venerated. With Louis cowering behind her skirts, she mustered her courage and answered, "One hundred and fifty years old." She tried not to smile.

Truth be told, she was thankful when the Lord of Life, like his prime minister, not only held his renowned temper, but laughed out loud. Anna felt herself relax a little. It was obviously the right way to approach the problem. Her relief dissipated though when he easily beat her at her own game: "In what year were you borned?" he asked. "In 1788, Your Majesty," she answered.[11] He looked at her for a moment, astonished. She couldn't tell whether he was annoyed or amused. Then, laughing uproariously, he demanded to know how how many grandchildren she had. Of course, Anna had no answer, and the king expected none.

But the king, surprised at her spunk and pleased at her imagination, had decided she would be suitable after all. He immediately began outlining her considerable duties:

> I have sixty-seven children. You shall educate them, and as many of my wives, likewise, as may wish to learn English. And I have much correspondence in which you must assist me. And, moreover, I have much difficulty for reading and translating French letters; for French are fond of using gloomily deceiving terms. You must undertake; and you shall make all their murky sentences and gloomy deceiving propositions clear to me. And, furthermore, I have by every mail foreign letters whose writing is not

easily read by me. You shall copy on round hand, for my readily perusal thereof.[12]

The scope of her responsibilities was scarcely pleasing to Anna. Sixty-seven pupils and countless wives were more than enough, never mind the crushing load of secretarial duties she would have to perform!

The question of her permanent residence was still unresolved. Imprudently, she made a fuss before the memory of the fiasco of her court presentation had dissipated. The apartments the kralahome had provided for her were more lavish than anywhere she had previously lived, but she did not want to be within his palace, shut up all night, with the possibility of permanent inclusion in his harem looming constantly before her. Anna appealed to the kralahome about her lack of privacy and independence, and it seemed to have some effect. But the result was unexpected, for the kralahome had decided it was time to teach the governess another lesson.

Anna had been delighted when, within a week, and at the king's express order, a furnished home had been found for her. She and Louis immediately set off after their guide, crossing the river by boat and following him down a long dirt road. At the back of a fish market so odorous the smell nearly suffocated all of them, the guide stopped. Three broken steps heralded the entrance to their new home. It was a typical Thai-style home, without kitchen or washroom. Surely the king did not expect her to take her baths outside on the steps to the river. Beebe was content to crouch outside, cooking on one of the little Thai charcoal braziers but Anna had expected a real kitchen. A broken table, two chairs and a filthy bed were the only furniture. Why, it was a throwback to the makeshift arrangements of her childhood in the garrison! Her first reaction was anger, but in a moment, Anna realized she had been outwitted once again.

Anna's resolve to win the upper hand only strengthened after her successive defeats; she swore not to rest until she had a decent house for herself and Louis, far from the prying eyes of the kralahome and the king. Perhaps her obstinance had something to do with the dire warnings of the American missionaries, who felt she was in danger of becoming part of the kralahome's harem. Harems were widely regarded by the European expatriates and the missionaries as dens of iniquity, where there was no concept of privacy. This in itself, she felt, would implicate her in what was seen as the nefarious, orgiastic goings-on within the harem. In their eyes, she was compromising herself simply by living at the kralahome's palace.

This episode may have contributed to Anna's difficulties in making friends with the Europeans living in Bangkok. She was hypersensitive to their criticisms, perceiving, perhaps rightly, that they saw through her manufactured stories about her upbringing. Nor did she know on whose friendship, advice and judgement could she rely; in fact, she had always been ferociously independent. Now, though, she was a mother and instinctively tried to protect her son from bad influences, real or imagined. She was less surprised than she was frustrated by the mocking, superior attitudes she perceived all around her, particularly those of the British, having been spurned by the consular staff, the merchants and their families. That left her with only the sailors, sea captains, and the American missionaries for company, and the king had practically forbidden her to associate with the latter group. None of these groups were particularly appealing, but at least the missionaries were less rowdy, and somewhat better educated. Although their religious prejudices were enormous, at least they weren't directed at her. King Mongkut had tried hard to keep her away from the missionaries' pernicious influence, but his efforts were futile. He had insisted Anna not live anywhere near the Protestant Mission, although the idea had been broached by Mr. Adamson when he proposed the terms of her employment.

The king was right about their zeal. Rev. Dr. Dan Beach Bradley never gave up trying to encourage Anna to a more active religious participation, but he also tried to use her as a tool for conversion of the royal family. The missionaries seemed to share her concerns about the unfortunate state of the Thai poor. At times, though, they were distinctly intolerant, reminding her of the self-aggrandizing British matrons and the sniggering officers of India. Both groups were convinced that their culture, habits and religion were the correct ones. Anna might have laughed at the way the British residents still clung so desperately to their silly class prejudices if she hadn't been so infuriated by them.

The charismatic Dr. Bradley was among the first batch of missionaries admitted to the country in the 1830s. He had brought the first Thai-language printing press to Bangkok, performed the first surgical operation and also administered the first vaccination against smallpox. But being a medical and literary innovator was easy in comparison with being a missionary. The missionaries had not counted on the Thais reluctance to forsake the passivity and gentleness of Buddhism for the burning hell fires and possibility of eternal damnation held out by Christianity. Even their attempts to barter medical treatment for attendance at religious meetings, and to pay local children to take religious instruction in English failed. Dr. Bradley's group were not successful in winning a single Thai convert.

Despite this interference, King Mongkut respected Dr. Bradley for his scientific interests, and rewarded him handsomely for his medical and educational achievements. The king's kindness did not keep Dr. Bradley quiet, though. If anything, his criticism of the heathen kingdom in which he lived, and of the king in particular, increased. Nor did King Mongkut try to censor Dr. Bradley's opinions as expressed in the *Bangkok Recorder*. Instead, he countered them with highly original defenses in his own newsletter, which he had printed on his English-language printing press.

Despite the king's encouragement of dialogue, diverse opinion and religious freedom, the missionaries managed to overstep the bounds of his tolerance. Shortly after he ascended the throne in 1851, King Mongkut asked some of the missionaries, including Mrs. Bradley, and Mrs. Mattoon, to teach English to his wives and children. They seized the opportunity to combine education with aggressive proselytizing; three years later, they found themselves banned entirely from the Palace.

In his haste to get rid of the women, the king had not been able to find a suitable replacement. It was several years before he discovered Anna, who was qualified and guaranteed to be non-converting.

Anna had no moral difficulties leaving religion out of education, to the delight of the tormented king. Little did he realize that Anna would prove to be a do-gooder of another sort, attempting to reform the entire and ancient Thai culture, concentrating her efforts on particular perquisites and pastimes of the monarchy. Her petitions on behalf of herself and others were plentiful and, by King Mongkut's standards, quite unreasonable.

Despite her crusading, the king was well pleased with her work, and did not fail to notice the attention she lavished on his children and wives, or the considerable affection they bore towards her. She had been in the palace for 14 months when tragedy struck her favourite pupil, who was also the king's favourite child. Somdetch Chowfa Chandrmondol, better known as Fa-Ying or the Celestial Princess, died on May 14, 1863, at the age of eight, a victim of the dreaded cholera which occasionally swept the country in formidable epidemics. Neither Anna nor King Mongkut could ever forget her.

A Royal Pain

It was five a.m. King Mongkut was on his way to the Gate of Merit, which would be opened shortly to admit the 199 monks who came each morning for food. He sat down on the straw mat beside his children, arranged in order of their rank. In spite of the abundance of his progeny, he never failed to notice the absence of one child. The Fa-Ying had been his favourite, and Anna's favourite, too.

Anna wrote later how at the child's deathbed, the normally dignified king

> Bitterly (…) bewailed his darling, calling her by such tender, touching epithets as the lips of loving Christian mothers use. What could I say? What could I do but weep with him, and then steal quietly away and leave the king to the Father?[13]

Anna had been nearly as grief-stricken as the king at the death of the sweet child. It was for her "courage and conduct" at the Fa-Ying's death bed that King Mongkut conferred an extraordinary honour on his normally irascible governess, elevating her to the status of Chao Khun Kru, or Lord Most Excellent Teacher. In addition, he gave her an estate in Lopburi and made her a noble. Despite her new position, Anna was just as outspoken.

Perhaps, the king thought as he walked, it had been a mistake to honour Mem Leonowens as he had. She seemed to think he had nothing better to do than to attend to her concerns about this slave or that wife or any one of a hundred other petitions she brought before him.

Yet, when he reflected on his "one great difficulty," he realized that she had gifts most people did not possess. She had inspired his children to learn English; she could converse in nearly as many languages as he could; and her skills in correspondence relieved him of many hours of work.

Unfortunately, Anna's romantic sense of right and wrong, so unflinchingly applied to perceived injustices in her adopted country, had grown. In the space of a few years, Anna had acquired countless "clients," as she called the hordes of people who begged for her intervention on their behalf with the king, the kralahome or some other official. Nobles and commoners alike stopped her in the streets or came to her house to seek advice or direct intervention. Anna soon perceived, correctly, that her clients' impression of her power was out of all proportion to her actual influence. Wisely, she made this mistaken impression work for, not against her. She knew that if the victims felt her influence was sufficient to help them, then those who had perpetrated the wrongs against them might also have an inflated sense of her power, and accede to her demands for reparation without her having to involve any Thai officials. It didn't always work. Anna often found herself imploring the king or the kralahome to intervene in particular cases, even when the law clearly was not on her side.

Although her desire to help the people who came to her for assistance was real, she failed to see that she was being manipulated by people who would not otherwise have had their cases heard. King Mongkut was more knowledgeable about the methods his subjects used to gain access to him, and he no doubt realized what was going on. But in Anna's activities he discerned an even greater threat.

To King Mongkut it seemed Anna's constant crusading was part of a nefarious plot to undermine him which was being nurtured by the American missionaries. He knew the missionaries nursed their resentment at having been categorically excluded from having any contact with the monarch's family as a result of their earlier attempts at conversion. He also knew they had not ceased trying to win royal converts, but had shifted their focus to attacking him personally in the English-language newspapers. Every time Mem Leonowens brought up another instance of wrongdoing on the part of government officials, or intervened in a grievance involving his household staff or one of his wives, he was sure the missionaries clapped their hands in glee. Indeed, his governess had the potential to make him look utterly ridiculous.

To King Mongkut it seemed that his governess took every opportunity to bring to his attention various moral, financial and physical wrongdoings wreaked upon his defenceless and utterly blameless subjects. They were hardly the sort of problems the king thought he should be dealing with, particularly when his attention was focussed on much more important matters of state. The French, who had long been intriguing against him with the restless Khmers, seemed poised to wrest the eastern provinces from his grasp. If the ever-rebellious northern provinces took advantage of the growing turmoil, the whole country might be overthrown.

In fact, King Mongkut had been under the impression he had specifically negotiated the end to such meddling by foreigners engaged to teach his children. He paid his governess well, in part as an assurance that the missionary problem would be mitigated. He made a mental note to remind Mem Leonowens of this fact the next time she ventured to ask a favour for this or that person, or attempted to stop a flogging because it offended her sensibilities.

Perhaps it was to reestablish his authority in the harem that the following incident occurred, virtually on the threshold of the school room. One of the king's wives, Lady Khoon Chom Kioa, was an inveterate gambler. Finally, the woman even gambled away the servants of her daughter, one of Anna's pupils, an act which enraged the king.

> Promptly the order was given to lash the woman; and two Amazons advanced to execute it. The first stripe was delivered with savage skill; but before the thong could descend again, the child sprang forward and flung herself across the bare and quivering back of her mother.
>
> *Ti chan, Tha Moom! Poot-thoo ti chan, Tha Mom!* ("Strike me, my father! Pray, strike me, O my father!")....
>
> The united strength of several women was not more than enough to loose the clasp of those loving arms from the neck of an unworthy mother. The tender hands and feet were bound, and the tender heart was broken. The lash descended then, unforbidden by any cry.[14]

He was royally sorry, though, that he occasionally lost his temper at the confounded English lady's continual intransigence. Why, she made him forget even Buddha's teaching, of which a prime precept was the avoidance of anger, and which he had faithfully observed for 27 years! Thoughts of the woman he considered his "one great difficulty" distracted him as he absently put boiled rice, fruit, cakes and siri leaves into the outstretched bowls of his brother monks.

As soon as they departed, he abruptly got up, bid a curt good morning to his children and walked stiffly toward one of his private temples, the Wat Sasmiras Manda-thung, erected in memory of his mother. He stayed longer than his customary hour in prayer and meditation, for the image of Anna's bustling form intruded into his thoughts even here. Two hours later, he relented and went to his private chambers for a nap. How much greater would have been his exasperation had he known that Anna had not hestitated to commit all of the embarassing details about the frailty of his temperament to paper.

He had succeeded in silencing her most persistent demand for her own house. In truth, the king was unconcerned about where the governess lived, as long as it wasn't anywhere near those infernal missionaries. He had provided elaborate apartments for her within his own palace as soon as she commenced her teaching duties. He simply could not understand why she was so dissatisfied with the arrangement, since similar accommmodation suited him and his burgeoning family perfectly. Yet she had been virtualy indefatigable in raising the issue at every turn. Time and again, she had reminded him he had promised her a brick house near, but not within, the palace grounds. The king denied that he had promised any such thing, only that he might give her a house or rooms within the palace. But in the end, and by sheer force of will, Anna managed to secure what she considered a proper house.

It was, typically, a hot afternoon as she sat in the shaded little balcony with a view of the winding Menam River, her little escritoire and writing tablet before her. She might have liked her home to be a little farther from the palace, so that it might not be quite so convenient for the king to summon her to answer his every beck and call, but the house was airy and cheerful. The house, which had been built only a few years before, had a small garden which overlooked one of the city's many canals. It was also unfortunately close to the king's favourite private temple, Wat Rajapradit, which gave him even further opportunity to send messengers with more correspondence for her to answer.

Yet she was fond of her house, and she particularly enjoyed sitting in front of its large dining room window overlooking her garden, hearing the sounds of the children splashing in the canal below. To her diary she noted, as she had faithfully since she had come to Siam, the events of the day. She was relieved to have a few moments peace, all the more so because the day had been particularly trying.

> When once the king was enraged, there was nothing to be done but to wait in patience until the storm should exhaust itself by its own fury. But it was horrible to witness such an abuse of power....[15]

Anna didn't even notice the touch of racism that had crept into her diatribe, unconscious of the influence of the tales about the king's cruelties which the British and Americans so joyfully propagated:

> Ah, if this man could but have cast off the cramping yoke of his intellectual egotism, and been loyal to the free government of his own true heart, what a demi-god might he not have been among the lower animals of Asiatic royalty![16]

But Anna had never met any other royalty, Asiatic or otherwise, and her experience of politics was woefully limited. That she or any of the other Europeans who so criticized King Mongkut had no yardstick against which they could measure their monarch was of little concern. In their eyes, he simply did not measure up. Despite her better judgement, Anna was too often drawn into the petty, backbiting and bigoted gossip that prevailed in Bangkok circles.

She fanned herself idly with a fresh frond of elephant leaf, but the effort it took produced no appreciable lessening of the intense heat which surrounded her like a wall. The humidity, coupled with the unseasonably heavy muslin dress she wore, had made her irritable. It was difficult to find any time at all to relax, what with teaching, answering the king's correspondence and his constant calls for her to attend him. Often, he summoned her just to argue over an English word which he had invented himself. Then there were the ladies of the harem who pestered her daily to assist them with their petitions to His Majesty. To them, no perceived injustice was too great or small to lay before the White Angel.

Yet she was frustrated by her inability to bring about any real changes. She had been so optimistic at first, taking a page from

Uncle Tom's Cabin and setting herself up as another Harriet Beecher Stowe. Surely there was something more she could do.

Perhaps there was. With that, she poured out her frustrations, bewailing the multiple misfortunes of Mongkut's many wives. It scarcely mattered that they were pampered almost beyond belief. When Anna looked at them she simply saw women who were not free, and lamented their condition in her finest descriptive fashion:

> How I have pitied these ill-fated sisters of mine, imprisoned without a crime! If they could but have rejoiced once more in the freedom of the fields and woods, what new births of gladness might have been theirs — they who with a gasp of despair and moral death first entered those royal dungeons, never again to come forth alive![17]

Then, her diatribe at a fever pitch, Anna reached a conclusion that was as startling as it was completely out of character:

> I had never beheld misery till I found it here; I had never looked upon the sickening hideousness of slavery till I encountered its features here; nor, above all, had I comprehended the perfection of the life, light, blessedness, and beauty, the all-sufficing fulness [sic] of the love of God as it is in Jesus....[18]

Of course, Anna didn't really believe what she had written, but it was exactly the sort of provocative language in which her reform-minded Victorian readers, especially Americans, would later revel.

On Liberty

"Ha!" he exclaimed to no one in particular as he paced up and down the audience hall. King Mongkut could not suppress a chortle of indignation at his governess's latest activities.

Anna was violently opposed to his supposedly barbarous handling of his wives. She had just told him in no uncertain terms she felt the women of the harem were treated only slightly better than slaves. He must remember to point out to Mem Leonowens that he had decreed some time ago that any of his wives, save the mothers of his royal children, could leave him if they wished.

"Ha!" he exclaimed again, this time startling one or two of the courtiers who had dropped off to sleep in the absence of anything better to do. He would also have to remember to tell her that so far, not one of his wives had done so.

Nor did her efforts to abolish what she called slavery cease when he provided her with a copy of the Siamese Slave Laws,[19] detailing the seven classes of slavery. He had even taken great pains to point out to her the exact mechanism by which a slave might be returned to freedom. Certainly he knew that no such provisions existed in America or anywhere else where much more brutal forms of slavery were routinely practised. Moreover, he was overseeing the gradual reform of the system to ensure that all traffic in human beings was eliminated in the country. The woman just would not listen.

Indeed, Anna was hardheaded on this question, pressing untiringly for reform. She would settle for no less than absolute and swift abolition of slavery, prostration and polygamy. She was surprised even at herself. Similar conditions had existed in India, and although she had felt disturbed, and even outraged by the British treatment of the Indian peoples, she had felt powerless to act. Now, it was as if something was awakening inside her. That the King had time and again professed to be dealing with these problems did not sway her from her path; she knew how slowly the wheels of change turned in Thailand, and she aimed to alter that, too.

Yet she was not entirely cynical:

> The capacity of the Siamese race for improvement ... has been sufficiently demonstrated, and the government has made fair progress in political and moral reforms; but the condition of the slaves is such as to excite astonishment and horror. What may be the ultimate fate of Siam under this accursed system, whether she will ever emancipate herself ... there is no guessing. The happy examples free intercourse affords, the influence of European ideas, and the compulsion of public opinion, may yet work wonders.[20]

The results of Anna's efforts were mixed, and earned her anything but universal affection. Some, like the kralahome's brother, (whom she believed responsible for two vicious assaults on her and her servants) were bitterly resentful of what they perceived as her growing power. But she was not successful in her pleas all of the time, like her most spectacular failure, Tuptim.[21]

As a child, Tuptim had been engaged to Balat, a boy from her village. He became a Buddhist priest, and Tuptim, because of her beauty and youth, was chosen to be part of King Mongkut's harem, the greatest honour a Thai woman could hope for.

But Tuptim was proud and despite the king's marked preference for her, she remained resentful and aloof, running and hiding from him at every opportunity. She soon ran away from the palace altogether, having disguised herself as a monk with the help of a trusted servant. She was noticed sitting in a temple by the head priest (and the king's favourite holy man), Chao Khun Sa. Seeking to help her, he turned her over to the care of another young priest of whom he thought highly for religious instruction.

To Tuptim's horror, the priest turned out to be P'hra Balat. Fortunately for them both, her former fiancé did not recognize her and she was able to continue the deception. For several months, it worked. Tuptim was happy simply to sleep at the feet of the man she loved. Yet she was putting herself and the priest at terrible risk. Simply for a monk to touch a woman, even by accident, was strictly forbidden.

But one morning, the inevitable happened. She overslept and was caught by the other priests as she dressed. It was a horrible degradation for P'hra Balat, yet he did not reproach her, or abandon her. Despite their innocence, both were accused of lewd behaviour and condemned to torture, then to be burned at the stake.

Anna's personal and heartfelt intervention with the king had no effect. Yet a month after the deaths of Tuptim and Balat, the king informed her he now believed the pair to be innocent. "I have much sorrow, mam, much sorrow, and respect for your judgment; but our laws are severe for such a crime. But now I shall cause a monument to be erected to the memory of Balat and Tuptim."[22] Anna had gained a small victory in making the king admit a mistake had been made. She failed to recognize that he had agonized over imposing the death penalty, although Thai law permitted him no choice. But it was still a tragedy that she had not had the power to avert. She could, however, console herself in her recent triumph, which took the unusual and unexpected form of Lady Son Klin.

School Days

Anna couldn't help but think how apt it was that every day she had to pass through Patoo Sap, the Gate of Knowledge, in order to enter Wat Khoon Choom Manda Thai, the Temple of the Mothers of the Free, where she held her classes for the young royals and their mothers. She was always grateful when she finally reached the tranquil orange and palm trees which fringed the temple and rendered the sun's blazing power nearly useless. She could see before she even entered the building that some of her more eager pupils had already gathered under the tall, gilded pillars of the temple. As Anna entered the temple, so did a retinue of servants, with pens, pencils, ink, books and slates for the day's exercises. Quickly, they lit tapers, and filled several vases with fragrant white lotus blossoms as an offering to Buddha, then padded off silently.

Among the pupils, as always, was Lady Son Klin. She was seated at a long, ornately carved table in the centre of the room, absorbed in her laborious translation of *Uncle Tom's Cabin* into Thai. Anna was always touched when she saw her most devoted pupil so hard at work. Every day, when she had finished her translations, she would sign her completed work "Harriet Beecher Stowe Son Klin." The two women had become good friends, but it had been difficult for Anna to win the confidence of the shy, beautiful woman whose name meant "Hidden Perfume."

Lady Son Klin had been out of favour with the king for years. Perhaps it was her tentative, withdrawn nature and her outcast status which attracted Anna to her, or the fact that her keen interest in learning had quickly made her the best pupil in the class. Anna really couldn't say for sure. Lady Son Klin's downfall had nothing to do with her behaviour. If anything, it was the fault of her Peguan ancestors for simply being, well, Peguan. She was descended from royalty, but her great-grandfather had been brought to Thailand as a hostage. Soon, though, his exceptional ability and status saw him placed in charge of the Peguan army corps.[23]

For nearly a century, the family had been responsible for the protection of Bangkok's upriver approach, and Lady Son Klin's father had been made Governor of Paklat, a river town. Despite the family's wealth (Lady Son Klin's father had given her son,

Prince Krita, a palace simply to mark the occasion of his birth), they were not favoured by the king, who was said to dislike all Peguans.

Misfortune followed Hidden Perfume everywhere like a monsoon cloud, and one day, she made a horrible blunder. Thinking she could secure for a relative an important government position through her own small influence with King Mongkut, Lady Son Klin sent her son, Prince Krita, with a petition to his father. Knowing his fondness for children, she hoped the petition might be granted. Unknown to her, the position had already been filled. The king was furious and accused her of being a spy and a traitor. The gentle Son Klin was beaten on the mouth with a slipper, considered among Thais to be a very degrading punishment for lying. She was then thrown in a dungeon. Anna appealed to the kralahome, and was once again successful.

Lady Son Klin was freed, and did not forget her friend's intervention, although it was really the prime minister she should have thanked. Presenting Anna with an uncut emerald ring from her own finger, she said, "By this you will remember the thankful friend whom you have freed."[24] The ring remained on Anna's finger for the rest of her life. But there was something else the wealthy royal lady, so concerned with virtue and piety, wanted to do, which would also please her new English friend enormously.

One auspicious day, Anna was invited to Lady Son Klin's home. To Anna's great surprise, she vowed, then and there, never to

> ... buy human bodies again, but only to let go free once more, and so I have now no more slaves, but hired servants. I have given freedom to all of my slaves to go or to stay with me as they wish. If they go away to their homes, I am glad; if they stay with me, I am still more glad; and I will give them each four ticals every month after this day, with their food and clothes.[25]

Anna's teachings had indeed had great influence. She felt a warm glow of pride at the actions of her most ardent pupil, and she could not suppress a sneaking feeling that she had been vindicated for all she had been through.

With the young Prince Chulalongkorn, destined to rule the country in a few short years, Anna would be able to claim even greater success.

Endnotes

1. *Halifax Herald, The.* "Her Farewell to Halifax: Mrs. A. H. Leonowens' Influence Liberated a Million Siamese Slaves," June 14, 1897, p. 6.

2. *Mongkut, King of Siam,* Phasa Angkrit, 1971, p. 8. It is not clear whether Anna's salary was quoted in US or Singapore dollars. In 1991, S $1.00 = US $0.55 or CDN $0.65. By way of contrast, her future son-in-law, Thomas Fyshe, received 50 pounds sterling per year in 1862, then about CDN $200.

3. *Ibid.*

4. *The English Governess at the Siamese Court, op.cit.,* p. 12.

5. Landon, Margaret, *op.cit.,* p. 18.

6. *Ibid.,* p. 19

7. *Ibid.,* p. 28.

8. Anna even described Moonshee as a servant although his status as pundit, or learned man, put him far above this. "Moonshee" or "munshi" is a Hindustani word which means, simply, teacher.

9. Indian servants were commonly treated with the utmost contempt by their British masters; harsh beatings for the mildest infractions were commonplace. Increasing racial segregation and British intolerance were blamed on the coming of British women to India, who were, apparently, appalled at the idea of sensuality around them, in the form of harems and erotic Hindu art.

10. It is impossible to imagine anyone demanding to be presented to Queen Victoria, or even Queen Elizabeth, out of turn.

11. *The English Governess, op.cit.,* p. 47

12. *Ibid.,* p. 48.

13. *Ibid.,* p. 97

14. *The English Governess, op.cit.,* pp. 114-115.

15. *Ibid,* p. 89.

16. *Ibid.,* p. 79.

17. *Ibid.,* p. 83.

18. *Ibid.,* p. 83.

19. In *Siamese Harem Life* (orig. published 1872, rpt. Arthur Baker Ltd., London) Anna gave a painstakingly detailed description of these seven classes of slavery, including the very straightforward mechanisms by which slaves, many of whom had bonded themselves because of debt. Keeping bondsman or indentured servants was a common practise in western countries, and was very similar to some of the categories of Siamese slavery, as Anna very well knew.

20. *Ibid.,* p. 238.

21. This story, minus Anna's involvement, is still known in Thailand today.
22. *Siamese Harem Life,op.cit.*, p.26-34.
23. The only permanent army forces were made up of prisoners-of-war and their descendants, who served four months annually.
24. Landon, Margaret, *op.cit.*, p. 136.
25. *Siamese Harem Life, op.cit.*, p. 204.

The Grand Palace, Bangkok, home of King Mongkut, his 600
wives and 67 (later, 85)) children.

Prince (Chowfa) Chulalongkorn.

Prince Chulalongkorn receiving instruction from an aged monk.

Chapter Two

Farewell to the Kingdom of the Free
1864-1865

The spirit of improvement is not always a spirit of liberty, for it may aim at forcing improvements on an unwilling people; and the spirit of liberty, in so far as it resists such attempts, may ally itself locally and temporarily with the opponents of improvement; but the only unfailing and permanent source of improvement is liberty, since by it there are as many possible independent centres of improvement as there are individuals.

John Stuart Mill[1]

"Ow. I'll get you for that! Buggerlugs! Villain! Ouch!" At the sounds of thumps and squeals, Anna rushed back to her school-room. It sounded like Louis, and it sounded like he was engaged in a boisterous round of fisticuffs with someone. But who? She drew her breath in sharply. If one of the royal children were to be harmed while they were under her care, His Majesty would never forgive her. There on the floor was a writhing, hissing pile of clothing. She clapped her hands sternly. "Up with you this minute, both of you. Now!"

Instantly, the pile transformed it into Louis and Chulalongkorn. Both boys looked rather sheepish, especially Chulalongkorn, who, although older than Louis by two years, apparently got the worst of the thumping. He was covering his left eye with his hand. "Let me see that," she said, her tone softening a little. The boy lowered his hand. His eye was swollen nearly shut. In a few hours it would transform itself into a huge purple goose egg, a reminder of Louis's quick temper. "Now, what was that all about?" she asked. Neither boy could answer. Already, the cause of their quarrel was forgotten, and Chulalongkorn was eager to escape his embarrassment. It was unseemly for a member of the Thai royal family to conduct himself so in public. The normally thoughtful, quiet and dignified little boy would have some explaining to do when his father saw him. Wisely, for his sake and for Anna's, he stayed out of his father's royal sight until his eye healed.

Yet Chulalongkorn never forgot the shiner given him by Louis, and later, he was often heard to laugh and re-tell the story of his beating at the hands of the smaller boy. Despite the immense difference in their backgrounds, Louis and Chulalongkorn became more than schoolmates; they became good friends, spending any spare moments together dreaming up new adventures. But even Anna didn't know how deep the bonds of affection would later prove to be.

It was hard not to feel affection for the young prince; Anna herself was quite taken with his intelligent and caring demeanor, although she suspected Louis saw a completely different side of him. Early on, Chulalongkorn had proved a valuable ally to Anna, and she confided to her diary that,

> He often deplored with me the cruelty with which the slaves were treated, and, young as he was, did much to inculcate kindness toward them among his immediate attendants. He was a conscientious lad, of pensive habit and gentle temper; ... Speaking of slavery one day, he said to me: "These are not slaves, but nobles; they know how to bear. It is we, the princes, who have yet to learn which is the more noble, the oppressor or the oppressed."[2]

Despite the number of women living around him in the palace, Anna couldn't help but feel the young prince craved a mother's attention; his own mother had died just before Anna's arrival in Bangkok. She couldn't help spending extra time with this solemn youth who, despite his richly jewelled clothing and sumptuous surroundings, was always concerned about those who had been born in less fortunate circumstances. She could only hope that one day he might lead the nation, instead of the person the king had selected as his successor, Prince Nooyai Nobhawongse, his eldest son by his first marriage.

She remembered talking to Chulalongkorn about the philosophies of Abraham Lincoln, whose honesty, forthrightness, and hatred of slavery she so admired. She could never forget one of the discussions, which had taken place in the study of Chulalongkorn's own charming palace, the Rose Planting

House.[3] He looked very thoughtful for several minutes, then declared,

> ... if he ever lived to reign over Siam, he would reign over a free and not an enslaved nation; that it would be his pride and joy to restore to his kingdom the original constitution under which it was first planted by a small colony of hardy and brave Buddhists, who fled from their native country, Magadah, to escape the religious persecutions of the Brahminical priests, who had arrived at Ayudia and there established themselves under one of their leaders, who was at once priest and king. They called the spot they occupied "Muang Thai" — the kingdom of the free ....[4]

Chulalongkorn was as good as his word.

Elephants for Abraham

"Mem Leonowens, I have a most brilliant idea."

"And what might that be, your Majesty?" Anna asked, only the slightest tremor of alarm creeping into her voice at the thought of what the imperial genius might have come up with this time.

"What your Mr. President Abraham Lincoln needs are elephants."

"Elephants?" Anna looked at her employer with genuine shock. It was true they had often discussed world affairs, particularly the American Civil War just then raging, so that King Mongkut was perfectly familiar with the legendary American president. It was also true that she had endeavoured to instill into the young Chulalongkorn the merits of Mr. Lincoln's violent opposition to slavery. But she had never mentioned Mr. Lincoln's name in connection with elephants, she was sure of it.

"Write this down," he commanded. Bowing her head to hide a smile, Anna poised her pen. She had long since given up trying to dissuade the king from acting on his often very original impulses. She had learned the hard way that it cost her more to fight him than it did simply to give in and do as she was bidden, however ridiculous it might seem. The king cleared his throat, then gazed up at the vaulted ceiling of the assembly hall for a moment. "It has occurred to us," he began,

> that if, on the continent of America, there should be several pairs of young male elephants turned loose in forest where there

41

was abundance of water and grass, in any region under the sun's declination both north and south ... we are of the opinion that after a while they will increase until they become large herds, as there are here on the continent of Asia, until the inhabitants of America will be able to catch and tame and use them as beasts of burden, making them of benefit to the country, since elephants, being animals of great size and strength, can bear burdens and travel through uncleared woods and matted jungles, where no carriage and cart roads have yet been made.[5]

No one was more surprised than Anna when President Lincoln, although engrossed in the intricacies of fighting a civil war, responded, and very courteously, too, on February 3, 1862. King Mongkut took the reply in stride as Anna read it out to him.

It seemed the idea had intrigued the American president. There just one thing wrong, which was explained so diplomatically in the letter that even Anna's touchy monarch could not possibly have taken offence:

This government would not hesitate to avail itself of so generous an offer if the object were one which could be made practically useful in the present condition of the United States. Our political jurisdiction, however, does not reach a latitude so low as to favor the multiplication of the elephant, and steam on land, as well as on water, has been our best and most efficient agent of transportation in internal commerce.[6]

The idea could have helped to surmount the tremendous obstacles faced by a young country attempting to conquer its far-flung territories and difficult terrain, save, of course, for the unfortunate fact that the North American climate was not at all compatible with the raising of elephants. Anna noted ruefully that had it been otherwise, King Mongkut's offer could well have changed the face of North America, although it might not have actually revolutionized the New World's transportation industry. She could hardly stifle a burst of laughter herself when she thought of her letters to Dr. Cobb, now back in Boston, being delivered by the American *elephant* express.

Siamese Harem Life

Beside many choice Chinese and Indian girls, purchased annually for the royal harem by agents stationed at

Peking, Foo-chou, and different points in Bengal, enormous sums were offered, year after year, through "solicitors" at Bangkok and Singapore, for an English woman of beauty and good parentage to crown the sensational collection; but when I took my leave of Bangkok, in 1868, the coveted specimen had not yet appeared in the market.[7]

—Anna Leonowens, writing in *The English Governess*

Anna twisted the diamond ring on her finger. The very thought of the thing made her uncomfortable. Why had the king really given it to her? Did he want to express something other than mere friendship? Surely he hadn't gotten it into his head that she wanted to be a part of his harem? The thought, once in her mind, would not go away. The more she thought about it the worse the implications of the gift, which even she had been ready to accept were innocent enough, became.

Certainly, his attitude toward her had changed in the weeks and months following the tragic death of the Fa-Ying. The gift of the diamond ring, for instance, the title and the estate. She knew it was ridiculous, but she couldn't help but wonder if the king didn't think perhaps he had found his English girl of good breeding, in the person of his governess. Horror of horrors. She could just see herself, busily chewing betel and reclining on some silk cushions, while she waited for his wizened old Majesty to pop along in his pyjamas. She laughed at her own whimsy, but there could just be a grain of truth in it.

There was nothing she could do but return his present. But how could she do it tactfully without incurring the royal wrath, sure to descend upon her even more violently than usual given the sensitivity of the topic. But at last, she had decided upon what she felt was the best method:

"Your Majesty," she explained, "I hesitated to accept so valuable a present, and now that I have had a week to think it over I have decided that I shouldn't have taken it in the first place. Of course, any time that you feel my services deserve an increase in salary—well, I should be very grateful for that instead."[8]

Only later did Anna wonder if perhaps she hadn't been a little crass in returning the ring, and asking for a raise in the same breath.

But King Mongkut accepted the ring back again without fuss.

He had to admit that he was genuinely fond of his governess. If she didn't want to accept his gift, that was up to her, although she had been acting a little strangely lately—and she seemed less irritable than usual. He had simply wanted to show her that he was magnanimous. Initially, he had found his governess rude and overbearing. She was simply so radically different from the multitudes of women who served him; sometimes, she seemed to have absolutely no desire to please him. On the other hand, there was no question that unlike many of his servants, Anna told him the absolute truth.

Moreover, Mem Leonowens was as fond of his children as he was, and had captivated their minds with her enthusiasm. For this he was grateful, and, indeed, he looked upon her son, Louis, with the same exceptional warmth he directed toward his own children.[9]

The Reclining Buddha

Anna pulled her cushions a little closer to the massive feet just above her head. She always felt a little like Gulliver in the land of giants whenever she came to visit the Reclining Buddha, whose astonishing gold image, nearly 100 metres long, filled the whole of a temple inside the huge Wat Po complex. Today, she had given herself over entirely to contemplating the elaborate mother-of-pearl characters on the Buddha's very large and very divine feet.

Her admiration for Buddha was unbounded, for he embodied the very ideas she sought to instill in her pupils. She mused to herself how much she had come to prefer the passive Buddha to the fire and brimstone rained down by Dr. Bradley and his ilk. Here, the end of the world was not imminent, and there was no threat of Hell, just the eternal peace which Buddha had sought and found. She recalled what her aged Thai teacher, a former priest, had told her about the prophet:

> His object was not only a religious but a social revolution. A good deal of what was venerated as religion he found to be merely social usage, for which a Divine sanction was feigned. [Buddha], without hesitation, rejected all of this…. His greatest blow to the old religion, however, was in his explicit repudiation of caste. He offered his religion to

all men alike.... Buddha boldly expounded to the people that, according to their own books, all men were equal.[10]

She would have to remember to impart that lesson to her students as soon as classes reconvened. Anna hadn't taught a class for nearly a month, and strangely, she had no desire to resume her duties immediately. She was glad to be able to recline here at all, for she was among those lucky enough to have survived the terrible scourge of cholera which had once again decimated the city. Anna herself had been very near death, so near, in fact, that the king had sent word to her bedside. She recalled, dimly, hearing some unknown voice read out his words as she lay confused and too weak to move. Should anything happen to Mam Leonowens, the voice intoned, His Majesty the Lord of Life would raise her son as his own.

Immediately, thoughts of Louis captive within the harem walls, silver anklets on his feet and wearing a gigantic golden crown popped into Anna's mind. She could never allow Louis to be taken from her. She must recover, if only to rescue her boy from the king's clutches. And she did. It was not long before she was up and hobbling around, with Beebe peering protectively over her shoulder to watch Anna's every move.

As a preventive measure, the king had taken his children and many of his wives away to his summer estate, and Anna had been left alone, with for Louis, to recover. Yet the blistering humidity of Bangkok continued to drain her energies and she spent her days in quiet contemplation, meditating, writing and reading in one of the numerous temples.

She reached for her writing tablet now as she sat in the cool dimness. Taking up her pen, she began to write in her elegant, firm hand:

> Often as I sat in the porches of these temples, the chanted prayers of the worshippers boomed through the aisles and inspired me with feelings of the deepest devotion; and whenever I passed along the dim, silent corridors, and came unexpectedly in front of one of the great golden images with its folded arms and drooping eyelids, looking down upon me in monitory sadness, with the wisdom of ages stamped upon its brow, amid the gloom of a never-ending twilight, while the head and shoulders were il-

45

luminated by a halo of light from the unseen source above, the effect was strangely mystical, solemn, and profound.[11]

It was still early in the morning, and a group of saffron-robed monks filed in past the huge form of Lord Buddha. Stopping in front of a small altar, they prostrated themselves three times, then sat down on the cool marble floor, as much to escape the fiery heat outside as to worship. Three young novices about Louis's age sat down behind their teachers. Anna smiled gently as she saw first one, then two, and then all three nod off to sleep in the cool calm of the temple.

She turned her attention back to the Buddha's feet. Did they contain any answers for her, she wondered. As she scrutinized the panels, each one symbolic of an episode in the Buddha's life, she couldn't help but cast her mind over the events of the past few years. How utterly her life had changed since she had left Singapore. No longer a scared young widow with scarcely an idea of how she would support her children in her penury, she had become a successful career woman of sorts. The work was difficult, and the king more often obstreperous than not, but she felt she had at last begun to earn his respect.

Anna reflected how, as the years had worn on, the king had begun to trust her, and had even come to depend upon her services. Yet like an old married couple, their relationship had continually grown more fractious the better acquainted they became. For years Anna had lived under enormous stress. Now, recovering from her near brush with death, she began to wonder if perhaps the price she was paying was too high.

It had become obvious that she had to stop working so hard. Even Dr. Campbell, the physician from the British Consulate, said so. In fact, he ordered her to cut her working hours in half, and Anna, who was still not her feisty old self, had complied with barely a whisper of protest. This new development, however, had not sat at all well with her employer.

Just then, Anna was startled from her long reverie by giggling nearby. She looked down to find the young novices had awoken from their naps, and were now stretched out near her, poking each other playfully. They had escaped, for the moment, the devotions to which the older monks were still attending. Anna smiled at them, and the youngsters giggled again. They had seen the White Angel here many times before, and had heard the many stories about her. Farangs were so odd, especially lady farangs with their strange headgear and odd, billowing bodies.

Anna got up a little stiffly from her cushions and smoothed her hoop skirt back into place. The boys giggled again at the sight, but she pretended not to notice. Her mouth burned with thirst and her head still felt cloudy. She wished Louis were here; it seemed a long way indeed back to her little home on the banks of a nearby canal. Taking up her cushions, she walked, a trifle slower than usual, past the tall chedis with their ornate ceramic decorations and the sculpted rock gardens of the temple compound. What indeed would the next few months bring, Anna wondered as she passed through the massive gates with their demon guardians, and turned down the avenue shaded by tall mango trees? Anna couldn't dismiss the nagging feeling that the period of peace she was now enjoying was merely the calm before the storm.

She didn't have long to wait. Shortly, she would find herself in the very eye of the tempest.

His Majesty's One Great Difficulty

"Truth is often stranger than fiction," but so strange will some of the occurences related in the following pages appear to Western readers, that I deem it necessary to state that they are also true.

— from Anna Leonowens' Preface to *Siamese Harem Life*[12]

The king was stomping up and down the audience hall. Crumpled paper was strewn everywhere, and it crunched under his feet as he marched. Anna, perched on a silk-covered cushion and balancing a writing tablet on her knees, looked at him unperturbed. She put down her pen. It was obvious the venomous mood the monarch had worked himself into would not dispel itself quickly.

Why, oh, why, had she stayed in Siam so long? Why did she continue to serve this glowering monster? Why, she wouldn't be surprised if next he ordered her toasted on a spit. Yet even as the thoughts poured out, Anna knew full well she was simply giving vent to her own frustration.

The king was given to fits of temper, but never to cruelty. Anna was often enraged by what she saw as his fundamentally different treatment of her because she was a woman. It seemed to her he was preying on her psychologically by asking his customary innumerable questions, plying her with work, and blaming her when things did not turn out exactly as he had envisioned.

In fact, the king was only trying to put a stop to her meddling by giving her more to do, but nothing worked. Not unexpectedly, Anna didn't see things in quite the same way.

She had expected only to be a teacher, and lead a quiet but lucrative existence. Instead, it seemed that nearly every waking moment of her life in Bangkok had become an epic battle of the sexes, and, ultimately, a clash of titan wills and wits.

Her nerves were already strained to the breaking point. And now there was this business of the treaty. It was more than ridiculous, it was positively outrageous! All she had tried to do was tidy up some ungrammatical and obscure wording, and she was accused of all manner of things! It was this unfortunate event, she was sure, which had led, directly or indirectly, to the scene now being acted out before her.

"Your Majesty," she began, "I ...."

"No! No! No!" He fairly shrieked the words. "Whyfore do you not write what I tell you? Whyfore are you so very, very obstinate? You are only a servant! You shall obey!"

It was August 10, 1866. Only a few months before, Anna had written to Sir John Bowring, the former British envoy to Thailand and a close personal friend of King Mongkut. The king wanted Bowring to be the new Thai ambassador to France, a delicate post which could only be filled by someone of the trusted diplomat's stature. Bowring's involvement was seen as crucial for the negotiation of a new Franco-Thai political and economic treaty. But negotiations had taken a decidedly hostile turn over which power would control Cambodia, historically a Thai vassal state.

But the letter had hardly even had time to reach Sir John in England when the king ordered her to write another one. He had changed his mind.

What irked Anna was not his inconsistencies, for she was used to that. What did irk her was that he expected her to say that it had been her own error, not the monarch's capriciousness. "Your Majesty," she exclaimed, her famous temper rising, "I'll consent to do nothing of the kind."[13] But King Mongkut, having changed his mind, could not see that he might endanger the close personal friendship Sir John bore him by revoking the appointment he had only just made. Instead, he vented his anger and frustration over the Franco-Cambodian negotiations on Anna. He did it in a way designed to humiliate her once and for all.

Late that same afternoon, the king's private secretary came to her house with a sheet of paper, listing numerous accusations against her. Among the accusations were that she had stolen a valuable Sanskrit book from the king's library, disobeyed his commands and thwarted his wishes, scolded him, shown disrespect, favoured the British Consul (whom the king did not like) over the American Consul, and so on.[14] The charges appeared trivial in themselves, but because they had been made by the king, Anna could be thrown in jail. This punishment would be waived if she simply signed the paper, thereby admitting her guilt, and sent it back to the king. She was also to write the letter to Sir John, as the king had instructed.

Once again, she flatly refused. But the matter did not end there.

The next day, when she tried to report for work at the palace at usual, she was met by a mob of soldiers and toughs with rocks in their hands. Anna and Louis were pushed and threatened with violence; Louis began to cry. Just then, a crowd of slaves which had been lingering around the palace gates came to the aid of Anna and Louis, edging them back through the gates to safety. No one was harmed in the incident, but it served to remind Anna that the king's will was paramount.

Anna discerned that her services would not be required that day, so she simply went home and waited. It turned out to be the best course of action.

Captain Bush intervened with the king on her behalf, and all was soon put right. But it was several weeks before she was again summoned to help the king's with his foreign correspondence.

This time, no one impeded her progress through the palace gates. No one, in fact, paid the slightest attention to her at all.

She climbed the steps to the king's audience hall and sat down at her usual table. She made no mention of the previous weeks' events, but her employer lost no time in speaking his mind:

> "Mem, you are one great difficulty. I have much pleasure and favour on you, but you are too obstinate. You are not wise. Wherefore are you so difficult? You are only a woman. It is very bad you can be so strongheaded. Will you

now have any objection to write to Sir John and tell him I am his very good friend?"[15]

She had none. Just the same, it had been a very trying experience indeed, and for Anna, the incident spelled the beginning of the end of her Siamese sojourn.

The incident was all the more unfortunate because Anna had developed a liking for Bowring. He was a born diplomat if ever there was one. The king liked him, too, and had signed a favourable trade treaty with the British based in large part on the personal esteem in which he held Bowring. On his first visit to Thailand, shortly after Mongkut had come to the throne, Bowring was not only given permission to sail his brig, *The Rattler* right into Bangkok, but allowed to fire a 21-gun salute in honour of the king. The unaccustomed display of power also had the effect of terrorizing the local people which was, after all, Bowring's ulterior motive.

Bowring had found the King to be charming, generous to a fault, learned and interested in the world around him; of course, he never saw him with his guard down, as Anna did. Yet he did get a glimpse of the painfully slow workings of Thai bureaucracy, which excelled at tying the most innocuous requests up in red tape:

> The Siamese were adept in their tactics of wearing down foreign nervous systems by constant procrastinations and delays. One day the Phraklang's father-in-law broke a favorite mirror, which so distressed the minister that he could not attend to the affairs of state for a whole day.[16]

At one point, talks over the British trade treaty threatened to become as protracted as Anna's quest for her own house and a rise in salary. Bowring, though, was a born diplomat; Anna was not. He never rose to the bait which managed to trap Anna every time: pride. He was a cooler player in the negotiations game than Anna, and managed to get almost every concession he wanted from King Mongkut, although not speedily.

The king, who loved to dabble with gadgetry, included in his sphere of interest new military technology. Finalizing the trade treaty with the British was put on hold while the king indulged his fixation with the shells and rockets carried by *The Rattler*. He asked Bowring, without the slightest embarrassment, for three shells and three rockets from the ships.

Contributing state-of-the-art British weaponry to the Thai arsenal was not what Bowring had in mind at all. But how could he refuse, without fatally compromising the trade talks, into which he had already put considerable time and effort? The answer was to compromise. The king graciously accepted Sir John's apologetic offer of one shell and one rocket, and was delighted with the results.

There were some subjects on which Anna and Sir John just didn't see eye to eye. It had been her continual and ineffectual quest to have the king agree to let her correct the grammar and punctuation of his English-language letters once dictated to her. The few times she tried correcting a word the king flew into a rage and accused her of distorting his ideas. Such an episode had occurred during Bowring's sojourn in Bangkok. The king lost no time in asking the envoy whether he thought his English grammar was of sufficiently good standards that he might send a letter in its unexpurgated version to Queen Victoria. Sir John wrote in response that the letter the king proposed to send, full of His Majesty's own colourful and inventive Anglicisms, would be not only be perfectly acceptable but "more welcome as the spontaneous effusion of Your Majesty's pen."[17]

Furthermore, Anna could hardly believe his response to the king's question about polygamy, a practice which Anna despised. Yet Sir John didn't quail. He told King Mongkut forthrightly that

> We are all bound to impart the education and habits and religion of those who differ from us. Lovers of truth are always tolerant, — and kind and generous in their judgment of others, — and I am persuaded there can be little truth where there is not much charity. —I wish Your Majesty much happiness in your many descendants.[18]

It was a wise response, for the Lord of Life had 600 wives whom he kept very busy. By the time Anna left his service, the royal heirs numbered 82 precocious little boys and girls.

"Mem Cha, Come Back Please!"

King Mongkut hemmed and hawed for six months, but finally acquiesced. He was dismayed that his governess seemed to want to leave him so badly, but her mind was made up. Anna was given permission to return to England in July, 1867 on sick leave. It was a well-deserved rest, for the years of unceasingly long, hard work had taken their toll. She had been ill with cholera twice, twice been attacked by unknown assailants, and been threatened several times. On top of this, she suffered from continual stress and overwork, and had nearly run herself into the ground trying to assist the flocks of people who poured out their troubles to her every day.

Anna noted testily that her long-deserved leave was only granted following "tiresome accusations of ingratitude and idleness...."[19] While six months seemed perfectly adequate to King Mongkut, Anna knew the voyage to England would take nearly three months each way. She intended to start her time clock ticking only when she reached her destination.

She yearned to see her young daughter again. Avis was nearly grown, and Anna knew she could never recapture the little girl's childhood years. Then there was Louis, who was becoming more and more rambunctious. He was already nearly eleven years old, and had received only as much schooling as she had been able to give him in her very limited spare time. The king made a fuss over him whenever he saw him and she was afraid Louis had already begun to get ideas into his head about the sort of life he wanted to live.

Anna knew there was only one thing to do: get him away from the tempting delights of the harem, which he was only just beginning to appreciate. She suspected, Chulalongkorn had been tutoring him in an all together too precise manner about the opposite sex.

It was the custom of British expatriates to send their children home for a proper education at age seven or eight. She knew the British residents of Bangkok found it strange she had not already parted with Louis, and she could no longer put off their inevitable separation. She had just the school in mind, highly recommended by her husband's relatives, Tom and Avis Wilkinson in Enniscorthy, Ireland. They were confident Kingston

School at Dun Laoghaire, Co. Dublin would be just right. It was said to be strict, and more importantly, it was inexpensive.

No one thought to consult Louis about his feelings in the matter. He had already made his mind up that he would not enjoy the experience. The headmaster, who had a penchant for beating boys into good behaviour, soon confirmed Louis's worst fears. School was not his favourite pastime, despite his mother's constant harping about his spelling and study habits. He was far more interested in riding, shooting, whooping, yelling and all manner of adventures than he was in sitting at a desk. Such a devil-may-care attitude would shape his whole life.

Only a few days remained before the *Chao Phya*, the ship which brought them to Bangkok six years before, would once again depart with the Leonowens's household on board. To Anna, those final days seemed like an eternity. She had already said her good-byes several times over, yet still the people came. She felt she must have embraced each of King Mongkut's 600 wives (which was perhaps more than he could say himself!) and certainly all of his children at least once. It was painful to see the little ones beg her to stay. She nearly wept herself when she saw their round and serious eyes on the brink of tears.

Chulalongkorn sent her a charming little note. It came on a silver salver, encased in a heavy blue velvet bag with his own seal embroidered on the outside. Inside the bag was another envelope, made of black silk but stiffened to the consistency of thick, handmade paper. This in turn was bound with a little gilded string. Inside, on a sheet of scented paper, he had written in his own beautiful handwriting and his perfect English, a personal goodbye. He wrote that he hoped she would have a pleasant voyage, and reminded her that she had had the honour of instructing him. Anna felt the tears well up in her eyes when she discovered the photo he had enclosed of himself, along with a gift of $30.[20]

Finally the day came for them to sail. There was a great commotion to and fro as the household goods were shipped off to the waterfront, trunks finally locked and the door to her dear house closed up. As they paddled down to the quayside, Anna took a long, last look at the city she had grown to love despite its intense heat, its intractable civil servants and all the worries and woes she had witnessed along its banks.

Louis acted as her guide to the city she already knew so well. He gave an own amusing running commentary as they passed the sheds which housed the magnificent royal barges; a little way down river loomed the stately magnificence of Wat Arun or The Temple of the Dawn. They passed the Portugese settlement with its large Catholic church, and after that, the old fort, which was Louis's favourite structure. He had scarcely a comment about Chinatown, or the Muslim mosque, but instantly recognized the home of Captain Bush, and sang out the names of the various foreign consuls occupying the houses further along.

He caught a glimpse of his mother's face. Today, none of his antics could make her laugh; she looked more sad and pensive than he could ever remember seeing her.

"Don't worry, Mama, we'll all be back soon, won't we? We'll live in a big palace all together, and eat rubies for lunch if we choose!" Finally, Anna managed a thin smile for her rambunctious son. He was always dreaming of pots of gold and battles with dragons. Boarding school would change him, she knew, but she wasn't sure she wanted him to be any different. His nickname, Quicksilver, suited him perfectly.

By the time they reached the quayside, dozens of people were waiting. Even the king turned out for the occasion, to her great surprise. Even more surprising was the solemn little speech he made to mark her departure.

Mam! you much beloved by our common people, and all inhabitants of palace and royal children. Everyone is in affliction at your departure; and even that opium-eating secretary, P'hra-Alack, is very low down in his heart because you *will* go.

He hesitated, and then a strange thing happened. The Lord of Life, the absolute ruler of his kingdom, attempted to publicly apologize to his governess:

It shall be because you must be a good and true lady. I am often angry on you, and lose my temper, though I have large respect for you. But nevertheless you ought to know you are difficult woman, and more difficult than generality. But you will forget, and come back to my service, for I have more confidence on you every day. Good-Bye![21]

He did not seem to realize just how much he had astonished his governess with his speech, and bustled off, distributing presents to the departing. To Louis, whom he had always liked immensely, the king gave the enormous sum of $100, a month's salary for his mother, to buy candy on the three-month voyage. Anna could only shake her head and smile at her employer's impulsive generosity. He would have consented to give Anna such a sum only after a good deal of argument about her virtues and discussion of her shortcomings, and her promise to repay it. Yet Louis never asked for money, for he never needed any, and that was precisely why the king constantly showered him with coins and presents. Anna couldn't help but think he was trying to drive home a subtle point: that if only she didn't bother him so much, he would be equally generous to her.

But it hardly mattered anymore. She had more presents than she could possibly make use of on the voyage, including fresh fruits and vegetables, clothing, bolts of material and other gifts of varying degrees of usefulness from her clients, all people she had helped in one way or another, plus the good wishes of her friends, the American missionaries.

Just then, the Chowfa Chulalongkorn was carried onto the quay. He jumped out of his magnificent palaquin, its elaborate golden surface shimmering under the blazing sun. As the crowd prostrated itself on the ground all around, he approached his former governess. They shook hands gravely. She knew that the significance, and, very likely, the finality, of her departure had not escaped the perceptive young prince, who could contain himself no longer:

> His regret seemed too deep for words, and the few he did utter were very touching. Taking both my hands and laying his brow upon them, he said, after a long interval of silence, *"Mem cha klap ma thort!"* —"Mam dear, come back, please!"[22]

But she never did.

Within the year, Chulalongkorn's life had changed utterly. The unexpected death of his elder half-brother, Prince Nooyai, in 1867, a few weeks after Anna's departure for Europe, cleared the way for Chulalongkorn to ascend the throne. Prince Nooyai had clearly been groomed for power, having held positions as superintendent of the garrisons of the Grand Palace of Bangkok, and also having acted from time to time as superintendent of public works. In 1862, following the death of his younger full brother, he was made superintendent of the Government Treasury. After the demise of the Second King in 1866, Nooyai was again promoted. At the time of his sudden death at age 44, he held the rank of military commander.[23]

Chulalongkorn was his father's third choice for the leadership. He was still too young to wield absolute power when he ascended the throne in 1868, and no one expected him to establish himself as an enlightened ruler, at least not right away. But Chulalongkorn knew the steps his father had already taken toward a more enlightened leadership, and he never forgot his earlier promise to Anna. In fact, he acted on it almost immediately.

On October 11 of that same year, he abolished prostration. It was one of his first actions as king. Four years later, having at last reached the age of majority, he set in motion the next phase of his plan to rule over a free nation, and began the process of emancipation of the various classes of slaves and debt-bondsmen. Anna wrote, in her customarily vibrant style that,

> When the wonderful tidings were actually proclaimed, the people listened as though they heard not; at best they distrusted the good report, and received the wondrous words as if they were merely the sounding of brass and the tinkling of cymbals in their ears...But when the 1st of January 1872 had actually arrived and they absolutely found themselves "free" men and women, their patient, loving hearts well-nigh burst asunder with joy. The glad cries of the ransomed millions penetrated the heart of the universe, and the "Despair" of the nation flapped her dark wings and fell down dead at the golden feet of the royal ransomer.[24]

After his death, King Mongkut would be praised by foreign visitors for having given his children, and particularly Chulalongkorn, a liberal education and familiarizing them with western civilization. Yet Anna could, and did, claim at least part of the credit. She was eternally proud that the beginning of her star pupil's reign almost immediately initiated a new era in Thailand still marvelled at today. For the young king, only 15 years of age when he began to fill his father's considerable robes, it was indeed an auspicious beginning.

Endnotes

1. John Stuart Mill, from the essay, *On Liberty*, written shortly after his retirement from the East India Company in 1859. Taken from *Prose of the Victorian Period*, ed. William E. Buckler, Houghton Mifflin Co., Boston, 1958, p. 274.
2. *The English Governess, op.cit.*, p. 238.
3. Although only about 13, Chulalongkorn was already deemed too old to live in the harem.
4. *Siamese Harem Life, op.cit.*, p. 220.
5. Landon, Margaret, *op.cit.*, p. 115.
6. *Ibid*, p. 116.
7. Actually, Anna left Bangkok in July of 1867. Anna Leonowens, *The English Governess at the Siamese Court, op.cit.*, p. 76.
8. Landon, Margaret, *op.cit.*, p. 187.
9. Ironically, while King Mongkut enjoyed Louis's continual questioning of everything around him, he did not like this same manner in the boy's mother.
10. *Siamese Harem Life, op.cit.*, pp. 6-7.
11. *Ibid.*, p. 196.
12. *Siamese Harem Life*, p. vi.
13. Landon, Margaret, *op.cit.*, p. 302.
14. *Ibid.*, p. 304.
15. *The English Governess, op.cit.*, p. 235.
16. *Thompson, Virginia. Thailand: The New Siam*, The MacMillan Co., (New York, 1941), p. 33.
17. Jumsai, M. L. Manich, *op.cit.*, p. 104.
18. *Ibid.*, p. 110.
19. *The English Governess, op.cit.*, p. 237.
20. This figure, and those which follow, are clearly in US dollars. The amount is listed in *The English Governess*, which was written for an American audience.
21. *The English Governess, op.cit.*, p. 237.
22. *The English Governess, op.cit.*, p. 238. It was characteristic of Chulalongkorn that he spoke Thai in public, even to Anna. Carl S. Bock, in his book, *Temples and Elephants*, (Sampson Low, Marston, Searle, & Rivington, London, 1884), observed that Chulalongkorn could speak and write English perfectly but that it was not his etiquette to speak in any language other than Thai (p. 17).
23. King Mongkut had settled on Prince Nooyai Nobhawongse, known as Kroom Mu'un Mahesuar Siva Vilas as heir apparent. Nooyai was King Mongkut's eldest son by his first marriage, before he became a monk. The circular states "… His Majesty considered him as his royal

Heir apparent or heir in his royal peculiar family." Unlike the British system, the eldest son was not automatically designated heir apparent. King Mongkut's letter, and the considerable responsibilities he had invested in his son make it clear Nooyai, not Chulalongkorn, was his father's original candidate for the leadership. Even so, the next king had to be approved by all members of a special government coucil. Angkrit, Phasa, ed. *Mongkut, King of Siam*, (Bangkok, 1971), from circular dated July 26, 1867, p. 33.

24. *Siamese Harem Life, op.cit.*, p. 221.

A temple building within the Grand Palace complex.

Wat Arun, known as the Temple of the Dawn, in Thailand.

Anna Leonowens in late middle age, possibly in preparation for her journey to Russia.

Chapter Three

New Horizons
1867-1887

"The villagers whispered among themselves that she was the ex-queen of Syria living among them incognito, and fabulously rich!"[1]

Anna got up from her desk and paced back and forth, the heels of her high, laced boots clacking sharply across the polished oak floor. She had been trying to compose another letter to King Mongkut, whom she had not heard from in some time. His uncharacteristic silence made her a little uneasy. She crumpled her half-written page in her hand, and resumed pacing.

She had already overstayed her leave, but she couldn't possibly go back until she had pinned King Mongkut down about a raise, and a reduction in the ridiculous number of hours he expected her to work. She could feel her blood pressure rising at the mere thought of it, and she resolved not to give in just yet. Anna sat down again at her desk and began to write.

Anna had left Thailand behind ten months ago and three continents away, but her conflicting feelings about the King still rankled her. He could be so tender and kind to his children one moment, and so imperious and demanding with her the next. The abrupt changes in his personality were just one of the things that infuriated her.

It was now May, 1868 and Anna was in New York. She should have left for Bangkok the previous November in order to be back in Bangkok before what she openly declaimed as a stingy six months' sick leave was up. But King Mongkut had been vague about increasing her salary in his last letter, and had said nothing at all about reducing her duties. Despite his evasion of what Anna considered the two major points of contention, he did seem to want his governess and personal secretary back rather desperately. He was even willing to give her a loan of $200. She was already getting $100 a month, plus a house rent-free, but Anna felt the king should pay her more for all the inconvenience she suffered, being called out at anytime of the day or night.

No, she thought, closing her writing pad decisively, she could afford to continue to wait a while longer. In any event, it would take four months for her reply, which was every bit as vague about the date of her return as the king's had been about her salary, to reach Thailand.

Anna drew her black shawl more tightly around her shoulders, and bent closer to the coal fire, rubbing her hands together briskly. She hadn't been warm once so far during her stay in North America, and it had been spring for nearly two months. Still, a bracing climate had been what the doctor ordered. The rain-soaked and newly-industrialized landscapes of England and Ireland of the previous September had not proved conducive to her physical recovery, although seeing her dear Avis, now nearly 14 years old, certainly improved her spirits.

She remembered the day, six long years ago now, when she had packed Avis off on the voyage to England, and herself and Louis off to Thailand. The six months' wait before she received word her daughter had arrived safely had been agonizing. So, too, had all the years apart. Despite the intervening years, Anna recognized her daughter instantly as she stood on the quay, as the ship to docked at Southampton. Avis was still as quiet and shy as ever, but she had grown into a decidedly attractive young lady with long, dark curls like her mother. At the sight of her, Anna could not hold back her tears. Her heart had nearly broken when she felt how tightly Avis clasped her when they met again on the quay side; then and there they promised each other they would never be separated for such a long time again.

The time the three spent together after Anna and Louis arrived in England was busy and brief. After a whirlwind visit to the Wilkinsons, her husband's relatives in Ireland, it was time to regretfully part with another child. This time, it was Louis's turn for boarding school. As much as she disliked being separated from first one and then the other of her children, she felt obliged not only to follow the established customs of the British middle and upper classes, but to see that they received the best educations possible under the circumstances.

Anna had no idea what sort of impression her son might have formed after living in such close proximity to the king's harem, but she was confident a stint at a spartan Irish boarding school would do him the world of good.[2] She reproached herself for not sending him away sooner, for she feared her selfishness in keeping him with her in Thailand may have deadened his interest in formal education altogether. Later events would prove her suspicions had been right.

By the end of October, with Louis settled but hardly content, Anna and Avis were bound for New York. Anna was eager not only to escape England's dripping mists, but to take up the kind invitation of Dr. Cobb and his bride, Katherine, to lodge with them in Boston for a few months. Anna shivered a little, and drew the shawl closer around her. She remembered when she first met Dr. Cobb. It had been in Singapore, and he lived next door to her and Leon. He had been a kind and attentive man, and it was through their mutual keen interest in literature and heartfelt belief in humanity that their friendship had first flowered.

But Dr. Cobb had opened Anna's eyes and mind to something else. An expatriate Bostonian living abroad for health reasons during the American Civil War, he fervently believed in the Yankee cause, with all its claims of equality and liberty. It was he who first filled Anna's impressionable head with popular stories of Confederate injustice and the evils of slavery. These same stories had already been effective in whipping up anti-slavery sentiment all over North America, and Anna's reaction had been no different.

How attentive Dr. Cobb had been after Leon's death, she thought, and how tenderly he had consoled her, reading to her from his own volumes of Harriet Beecher Stowe, Nathaniel Hawthorne and Ralph Waldo Emerson.

Anna had been a good student, for she identified with the heroes and heroines who had so dramatically triumphed over adversity. She couldn't help but feel that she, too, should somehow fight against the intolerance and injustice that she had personally suffered, and witnessed all around her. She found her cause in Thailand, and took every opportunity to rail against oppression, perceived and real, and to spread the word about the evils of slavery to her impressionable pupils.

The issues that had driven the U.S. to civil war were much more complex, as were the practices of slavery and harem-keeping in Thailand, but like Dr. Cobb, Anna had been able to reduce these issues to their simplest and most easily understandable forms in order to arouse the greatest popular sentiment amongst her pupils.

By the time she debuted as an author several years later, she had mastered the technique.

Not long after Anna's inconclusive exchange of letters with King Mongkut, mother and daughter briefly left New York City for the remote isolation of the Catskill Mountains. Anna's dark skin, its natural colour heightened by the tropical sun, and her comical hoop skirts soon had the countryside abuzz with rumours that she was the queen of Syria! Once again, she had managed to attract the attention of the locals without lifting a finger, inspiring gossip about her unusual appearance, eclectic baggage and strange habits, all of which she seemed little inclined to change.

But the clean, cold air had its desired effect. Not only was her health restored, but Anna's literary creativity was focussed. There in the Catskills, about a year after her arrival in the United States, she began to write the account of her life in Thailand that would so asonish her readers.

Meanwhile, back in Ireland, the 13-year-old Louis was getting edgy. Many months had passed and no date had been fixed for his mother's return to Thailand. Stuck in his second class boarding school, he made it clear in letters to his mother that he did not want to be left out of another adventure. No doubt he compared his situation to that of his sister's, fearing that what had been held out to him as a temporary situation might just become permanent. Avis, after all, had been stuck in a boarding school for six years without so much as a visit from her mother or her brother.

On April 28, 1868, Louis attempted to convince his mother (in a letter of such atrocious quality that she must surely have been shocked) that if she went back to Thailand she would need his services to protect herself against a curious combination of foes, including priests, cows and French people.

But Louis worried for nothing. There would be no return to Thailand.

On October 1, 1868, King Mongkut died. He had contracted a fever while leading a group of French scientists and other dignitaries into the southern jungle to view a solar eclipse which he had predicted, rightly, would fall on August 18. The 15-year-old Crown Prince Chulalongkorn suffered the same fever, but recovered and was immediately elected King.

On November 25, Anna heard of King Mongkut's death and immediately wrote to her former pupil, now King Rama V. It had taken less than two months for the news to reach her, instead of the usual four. Chulalongkorn replied on March 6, 1869 in a warm and cordial letter. Paradoxically, the boy who had begged his governess to come back to Thailand did not take the opportunity to invite her to serve the royal family once again.

March 6, 1869
To *Mrs. A. H. Leonowens, New York*

Dear Madam

I have great pleasure in condescending to answer your sympathising [sic] letter of 25th Nov. last wherein the sorrowful expressions of your heart in relation to my most beloved Sovereign Father in demise which is a venerated burden and I have felt to this day and evermore shall bear this most unexpressible loss in mind, with the deepest respect and lamentation, and resignations to the will of divine Providence; —are very loyal for you two toful, and share your grief in behalf. The affection you have for your royal pupils, and the kind remembrances you have made of them in your letter, loves you too with that respect and love your are held in their esteem ... I have the pleasure also to mention you that our Government in council has elected me to assume the reins of Government notwithstanding my juvenility, and I am pleased to see the love the people have for me, Most undoubtedly, arising from the respect and veneration they have had for my beloved royal Father, and I hope to render them prosperity and peace, and equal measure, they have enjoyed since the last reign. In return, May you and your beloved children be in the peace of the divine Providence.
I beg to remain

Yours Sincerely,
Somdetch Phra Paramindr
Maha Chulalongkorn
Kluw Chowfa Kwa
Supreme King of Siam
on 114th day of reign.[3]

In Anna's mind, the death of her employer and the certainty that she would not return to Thailand cleared the way for her to reveal all her incredible experiences to a reading public eager for news of the world.

The Legend Begins

"Mrs. Leonowens, truly, your stories are wonderful. We are considering them for the spring and summer editions. I hope you will be very pleased."

James Freeman Clarke, editor of the prestigious American magazine, *The Atlantic Monthly*, pushed his visor back a bit and scratched his head thoughtfully as he looked at his newest, and certainly most exotic, correspondent. "How on earth did you ever land in such a place as that?"

Anna hesitated. Dr. Cobb had warned her the question was likely to crop up, but she wasn't entirely comfortable just yet with some of the details of her background as she had mentally altered them. "Well sir," she said, "that is entirely another story." Mr. Clarke looked up, amused. "As you wish."

Later, Anna allowed herself a sigh of relief that the magazine editor had not questioned her too closely about the unusual circumstances which had brought her to the attention of the Thai king. If examined too closely, she knew, her background might not prove up to snuff. The editor, though, had read between the lines of Anna's lively, direct prose, and saw something more: magazine sales.

Anna welcomed the sale of four articles to *Atlantic Monthly* — and not just for the publicity it would bring her as an unknown writer. She needed the money. Although she had saved a considerable part of her salary as the royal governess, the years before the publication of her Thai tales in April, May, June, and August of 1870 had been frugal ones. She had no idea when, or if, she would ever have more money coming in, and she hoarded every penny. She had even taken up teaching school again, this time on Staten Island, with Avis as her trusty assistant. Louis, for the time being, remained in boarding school, but regularly wrote plaintive letters begging for his release.

Soon, though, he had had enough, and mustering the sort of resourcefulness his mother would have shown in similar circumstances, somehow got himself across the ocean to New York. The Irish boarding school experience had soured him on education entirely, and he worked at a succession of jobs in New York, and throughout the States.[4] Anna began to despair that her son would ever settle down.

Anna counted the publication of her stories in 1870 as a moral victory. Not only had she become a published author, but she had once again proven a woman could earn her own living, and a good one at that.

Initially, the lack of information about this talented new author only created an air of mystique and a demand for additional copies, but Anna — and the details of her early life — would not remain obscure for long. The stories themselves generated terrific interest and an intense curiosity about their author. Anna was poised on the brink of fame.

The timing couldn't have been better. Anna was well satisfied with herself and the tales were gathered together and embroidered into the fabric of her first book. The very same year, her purportedly autobiographical *The English Governess in the Siamese Court: Recollections of six years in the royal palace at Bangkok* was published. It was dedicated to Mrs. Katherine Cobb, and it marked the birth of the legend of Anna.

But Anna was very nearly overwhelmed by the radical change in her fortunes brought about by some simple tales. Suddenly, people wanted to meet her, talk to her about her experiences, and know every detail of her life. If the former army rat felt any desire to reveal her true origins, or the circumstances of her miserable army upbringing in near-poverty in India, she thought the better of it. She became, firmly and forever, Mrs. Anna H. Leonowens, former governess to the Court of Siam, widow and daughter of British officers, who had tragically lost her fortune in a banking scandal and had been condemned to a working life in order to support her young family.

Work she did, diligently churning out stories in an effort to match her first runaway success. Two years later, her efforts were rewarded by two more articles in *Atlantic Monthly*, "Favourite of the Harem," and "L'Ore, the Slave of a Siamese Queen." They were soon expanded into her second book, *The Romance of the Harem* (later published under the title, *Siamese Harem Life*) which, much to Anna's delight, also created a sensation. The effect was precisely what she had intended, for the book relied even more heavily on the somewhat imaginative and unfortunate theme of her first book: injustice and cruelty, particularly towards women. The chivalrous sensibilities of the Victorian era had been aroused, and readers, fascinated and outraged, made their feelings known by buying copies.

Anna was able to parlay her success onto the profitable lecture circuit. Her calm, confident bearing, her excellent speaking voice, her astonishing knack for detail and gift for description and her exotic background combined to ensure her popularity for several years to come. Anna quickly found herself with an entirely new circle of friends.

That year, she met John Paine, an eccentric and rich old man, who enjoyed literature and had been fascinated by her book. They appeared to have hit it off, because she spoke often of visiting the old man at his homes in New York City and in Newport, Rhode Island. Her life and travels as well as her abilities fascinated him, and he enjoyed listening to her one thousand and one stories. They discussed dozens of subjects at length, and she read to him the latest books as he suffered from poor eyesight. In short, Anna provided Mr. Paine with something his money could not buy: friendship. She was rewarded, in turn, not with money but with something even more valuable: introductions to the elite of the New York arts scene.

Anna, it seems, had an uncanny knack of appealing to exactly the sort of person who could help her the most: Mr. Adamson in Singapore, who recommended her to the king; Dr. Cobb in Boston, who helped secure a publisher, and now Mr. Paine. Thanks to his influence and her own ability to maximize an opportunity when one presented itself, Anna swiftly became the city's latest literary phenomenon. She met many of the most popular New York-area writers of the day, including Oliver Wendell Holmes, Henry Wadsworth Longfellow, Julia Ward Howe, Ralph Waldo Emerson, but for Anna, the most important of them all was Harriet Beecher Stowe.

Long afterwards, Anna cherished the memory of that day in 1872 when she was finally introduced to the writer who had been her inspiration, shaping from afar her actions, outlook and writings. Anna found Mrs. Beecher Stowe to be "a strong but plain woman, very handsomely dressed," yet she was very nearly overwhelmed with emotion when her idol, who had evidently read Anna's works, "embraced her as if she had known her for a lifetime."[5] She could not have hoped for greater praise.

Her son was another matter. Louis had obviously inherited wanderlust from his mother and father, and Anna, now a busy writer and lecturer, could no longer lavish the attention and companionship of former times on her son. He finally emigrated to Australia, where he worked the gold mines for several years. It was rumoured that he had been imprisoned, although this charge was unsubstantiated. A few years later, having decided to come back to America, he asked his mother for money to pay off his debts. Anna declined.

It was probably the best thing she could have done for him. Louis, every bit as resourceful as his mother, didn't give up. By 1881, he found himself on the long and winding road back to his boyhood home in Bangkok. His old chum, now King Chulalongkorn, welcomed him back. More importantly, he gave him a job.[6]

Enter Thomas Fyshe

Avis and Anna sat on the deck of the Staten Island ferry, enjoying the cooling Sunday afternoon breeze blowing over them. "Mama," ventured Avis in a timid voice, "Mama, there's someone I'd like you to meet." Anna turned to her daughter, who trembled a little before her mother's penetrating eyes, and knew the moment had come when they might soon be separated.

It was inevitable, of course, that Avis would marry. She was intelligent, beautiful and hardworking. Since Anna had opened her little school on Staten Island several years ago, Avis had worked with her tirelessly, dedicating herself to little else besides pleasing her mother. It was arranged that Thomas Fyshe would call the following Sunday.

Anna was not at all disappointed when she met Avis's young man, an intelligent and ambitious Scotsman.[7] In fact, they took to each other instantly. The perceptive Anna knew a good match when she saw one, and she could tell the young couple were in love. She had no reason to oppose the liaison. The shy, eager-to-please Avis no doubt heaved a sigh of relief.

But in 1875, the path of their courtship took a sharp turn to the north, when Thomas was offered a position as manager of the Bank of Nova Scotia's Saint John, New Brunswick branch. Within the year, he replaced the man who hired him and took over as cashier of the flagship Halifax branch when his mentor resigned due to ill health. It had been a stressful time at the bank, occasioned by the discovery that another cashier, James Forman,[8] had embezzled more than $300,000, wiping out the bank's

$80,000 reserve fund. The effects of this tremendous scandal were felt for years afterwards.

It was left to the neophyte to sort out the mess, and re-build the bank on a solid financial footing. His difficult task was made harder by the sorry shape of the Nova Scotia economy, which had been in a steep decline for some time. The end of the American Civil War in 1865 had dried up Nova Scotia's sure market for its unskilled labour. An estimated 10,000 Nova Scotians fought against the evils of slavery in the Yankee army, but now that the war was over, the spectre of unemployment was beginning to rear its head.

Mrs. Leonowens, he knew, would certainly have approved of the Nova Scotian soldiers' strong stand against slavery. But he would also have to tell her about the excited and naive young men, eager to see something of the world, who were lured away from home by the $300 bonus offered by unethical Union recruiters. She had supported the war, but deplored its violence.

The distance separating him from Avis only caused his heart to grow fonder. The June 27th edition of Halifax's *Acadian Recorder* noted the marriage at Athos Memorial Church in New York of the 33-year-old Fyshe and the 24-year-old Avis on June 19, 1878. Adhering strictly to custom, Anna insisted that the marriage announcement contain no mention of her, only of the bride's late father. It was uncharacteristic that Anna should miss an opportunity to publicize her accomplishments and her books. By July 2, the couple had departed for Britain. No doubt one of their most important stops would be in Scotland, where Thomas would present his bride to his family.[9]

But all too quickly, the delights of the honeymoon, including the perfect isolation they had enjoyed aboard the ship, was over. It would be some time before Thomas and Avis could ever be so completely alone again.[10] Part of the reason was Anna.

Avis hadn't forgotten the promise she had made that day long ago on the quay side to her mother: Anna and Avis were a package deal, and even marriage would not separate mother from daughter. Anna, who would prove to be a most unusual mother-in-law, soon joined the happy couple in their first home, the cozy Hillside Cottage, located just outside Halifax, and overlooking the tranquil Northwest Arm.

It would be the start of a new life for them all, a life upon which Anna impressed her own distinctive stamp. Mindful of her new ranking on the social ladder (which she had begun to ascend in earnest in New York), she modified the wild Bangkok social crusades that had become so magnified in her books, and in popular imagination. During her New York years, she had learned the art of tact, metamorphosing once again from an English governess to a famed literary lady, whose Oriental scholarship was well-nigh peerless.

Anna's books had sold well, and she commanded a good fee as a lecturer. But the royal wages she had earned a good 10 years before had long been spent. It was, therefore, a relief that her daughter had married so well. Thomas was well able to provide for them and the brood of eight children. Moreover, the move north brought Anna into a ready-made position within the elite of Halifax society, by virtue of her son-in-law's prominence, and her own spreading fame. Before long, she had virtually usurped her timid daughter's place at the side of Thomas Fyshe. Avis, in spite of herself, was relegated to running the household while her mother and husband became the talk of the town.

Although it was fashionable for the upper classes to moralistically and unilaterally reform the lives of the downtrodden, Anna never fell into this trap. She abandoned the confrontational approach that she had used in Thailand in favour of a concilatory, consensual approach. Everyone around her remarked on her attitude of true caring and charity. The same could not be said at home, where she had turned into something of a domestic tyrant.

Anna found her Canadian surroundings much more rudimentary than those of sophisticated New York. Halifax at the time was a city of only 31,000 people and 4,000 houses. Anna found the citizens very proud indeed of their 60-bed Civic Hospital, their courthouse and jail, their Home for Aged Ladies, their new Masonic Hall, the three homes for orphans, the YMCA and so on. (Oddly enough, the Poor House was not only the pride of the city, but its tallest building at nine storeys. It was destroyed by fire 1882.)

With 33 churches within the city boundaries, the civic emphasis leaned heavily towards the spiritual. Education, by and large, was sorely neglected; there were only six schools in Halifax when Anna arrived. Many people simply could not afford to send their children to school, and they depended upon the wages their children earned.

The plethora of other charitable institutions undoubtedly relieved the burdens of providing health care and temporary shelter to some degree, but by and large, the poor still lived miserably. There would be ample opportunities for Anna to come to their aid.

As the self-appointed elder stateswoman of the Fyshe household, Anna indulged her vigorous interest in social justice for women through a variety of causes, clubs and charities. With the support of like-minded Haligonians, Anna spearheaded prison reform, founded schools for the blind, reading clubs and an art college, spoke out against truancy as well as other problems of the day.

In a sharp departure from her Bangkok days, she stopped short of demanding a new social order. Like most well-off Victorians, she felt obliged to look after the poor but she no longer seemed to possess the same desire to help them climb the social ladder. Perhaps Anna was already learning to moderate her opinions according to the company she was keeping.

Slavery at Home

> Her first glance was at the river, which lay, like Jordan, between her and the Canaan of liberty on the other side.
> —*Uncle Tom's Cabin*.[11]

"I have defended, advocated, and gloried in the liberty of other men; I have never defended my own. I have simply taken it and used it."[12] Anna could almost hear Henry Ward Beecher's thundering voice as she read over the newspaper article reprising one of his more famous sermons. She had once heard the famous reverend speak, and it had seemed to her on that occasion, like a latter-day Joshua he might bring the walls of the theatre tumbling down even without a trumpet.

He had left a strong impression on Anna. She liked his oratorical style every bit as much as that of his sister, Harriet Beecher Stowe. She felt a certain kinship with them both; they felt the same way about many things. "My study and my sympathy have been toward my fellow man," Rev. Beecher had declared, "and whatever I thought would do good I have preached, and whatever I felt to have no usefulness in it I have neglected, whatever the church may have done."[13] A bold statement, perhaps, but Anna could well fathom the sentiments that lay behind it: she had done exactly the same thing. Anna had embraced various religions, but had never been enslaved by them. She had tried to do good when she could, and had tried not to be held back by bureaucracy and prejudice.

Anna's first two books, which their anti-slavery message, couldn't have been published at a better time. Abolitionist sentiment was still running high in the U.S. and Canada, thanks to the efforts of Reverend Beecher and his colleagues. In Nova Scotia, the revulsion towards slavery had made it easy for Union army recruiters to marshall support. In the end, the American Civil War had been won by the abolitionists, and slavery was ended in the United States.

Reverend Beecher then looked beyond North America to root out injustice, calling relentlessly and eloquently for an end to slavery everywhere. His fellow preachers in Nova Scotia and elsewhere soon took up the call, in a slightly modified form; Nova Scotians had given up their slaves 40 years before.[14] His righteous quest was aided immeasurably by his sister's book, *Uncle Tom's Cabin*; those who had not already learned it virtually by heart were reading about it, or talking about it.

They were still talking about it by the time Anna's books were published, but her stories added exotic new elements to the popular outcry against slavery. Unlike many of her compatriots, Anna could already point to the record of her accomplishments in Thailand and show real change had begun.

But the ministering White Angel had changed her style since Bangkok. The perilous and personal charitable rounds from which the poor and unfortunate of that city so benefitted had been given over in favour of committee work and delegations to the mayor. Although she worked tirelessly, and possibly even more effectively than ever before, the slum of Africville, long considered Halifax's disgrace, does not seem to have lain within her particular parish. If it did, she did not take up the cause of its black residents in any visible way. The crusader who fretted that the blind might not be able to ever experience the joys of reading recorded no denunciation of the deliberately poor or non-existent educational system for blacks. That generations of Africvillers were seen by the white majority as fit only for a lifetime of menial tasks, at subsistence wages[15] in abominable living conditions did not raise any written protest from Anna Leonowens. If she witnessed the humiliating sight of a local black man acting as a target for baseball throwers at a carnival, she kept silent. The man wound up with a broken collarbone.

Freedom itself was a moral dilemma; the lives of the working poor were brutal and harsh before the invention of universal social programs. Such people relied on the benevolence of the upper classes as much as they might have upon any master. Often, poor black and white Haligonians alike wound up in Rockhead, the city prison, convicted of stealing, prostitution or other crimes. Sometimes, this was more by design than by chance, and it was not unheard of for habitual criminals to petition the court to be incarcerated for the winter. Incarceration had a benefit that Anna had not considered. Unlike freedom, jail at least came with regular meals and a relatively warm bed.

Her move to Halifax had brought Anna more than a comfortable home and a framework within which to continue her social crusading. Avis' first pregnancy inured Anna to a new idea, and one which she came to value as her life's real work: the education of her grandchildren. But that didn't mean her travels were over — not by a long shot.

Moscow

The lecture room of the Church of England Institute was filled Tuesday by a most appreciative audience, in spite of the pouring rain, to listen to the lecture of Mrs. Leonowens on Russia...."

Halifax Morning Herald,
April 26, 1894

It was 1880. The undulating Russian steppe wound endlessly before her as the train rumbled its way to Moscow. But Anna was not off to another teaching job. This time, she was on assignment as a journalist, travelling alone through the vast but troubled country, still convulsed in the aftermath of the assassination of Czar Alexander II.

Anna had been invited to make the trip by the popular *Youth's Companion* magazine to write about the changes sweeping the nation. She had accepted the assignment with great gusto, despite having recently celebrated her forty-ninth birthday. (Her family thought she was celebrating her forty-sixth.) That she was selected for the assignment, ahead of the dozens of male journalists thirsting to conquer the steppes of Russia, was testimony not only to her continuing literary fame but to the sheer force of her writing skill.

She proved to be an excellent choice. Any concerns the editors may have had about sending a middle-aged woman alone across Russia were soon put aside. Anna proved herself adept at traversing the country, sending back fascinating reports. She also appears to have picked up several Persian carpets by haggling in Hindustani with the astonished vendors.[16]

It was a dangerous time, and she knew it. She could not avoid the intense scrutiny which dogged her everywhere she went; Anna was said to have been the first foreign women to travel alone through Russia. Her mere presence in the country aroused suspicion that she was a spy. She had even been assigned two government bodyguards for her own protection. Anna knew the real reason they did not let her out of their sight was that they suspected she was fomenting some sort of Nihilist plot to rid the country of its monarchy forever.[17]

Although Anna cultivated no special interest in monarchies herself, it was odd that kings and princes were a recurring theme in her life. All the same, she had admired Alexander II for freeing Russian serfs, even if he had not had the purest of motives:

> It was, without doubt, the result of the Crimean War. The Czar determined that Russia should have an educated army; that every soldier should understand military instructions; and fight with the same intelligence and skill as did the English and French soldiers. To this end, forty millions of an almost unlettered peasantry were freed, and the government began the work of educating her millions.[18]

Despite this reform, she was sure popular uprising was inevitable, and said so in a letter to Avis remarkable for its precognition:

> One day there will be in Russia a sudden revolution of the most fearful character, for the greater part of the people are savages still. The government is infested by a deep corruption, the Nihilists consider the Czar the root of all evil and his destruction the first step toward national life.[19]

Thirty-six years later, her prediction came true, as revolution swept Russia into a new era.

Yet the Czar's decree engendered a secondary effect which Anna applauded wholeheartedly: the establishment of schools all over the country, where communal villages sent its young men and women to be educated, and later to train as teachers. She marvelled at the young women students, scarcely able to contain her admiration for their boldness and freedom, although she would hardly have condoned such free-thinking in her own grandchildren:

> There is no more interesting figure in Russia than a lady student. She generally has her hair cut short, her dress is almost like a Quaker's in its quiet tones and extreme simplicity. She is invariably a thorough musician and passionately fond of music, and they are one and all inveterate smokers....I have met them in groups on moonlight evenings, seated in some picturesque garden nook, smoking in quiet, pensive thought, regardless of everything around them, and there is nothing more touching than their air of settled sadness.[20]

Yet Anna's sympathies were firmly with these determined young women, who had often made great sacrifices in order to obtain their educations:

> I learned that not a few of these students were girls of noble family who had broken away from home, and were studying under assumed names. The difficulties which some of them have had to contend with to obtain even the privilege of college education reads more like a chapter out of a romance than as belonging to our work-a-day world.[21]

Anna's own life had contained great dollops of romance and exoticism; her own story had held a whole continent transfixed. She recalled, when she saw the young female students smoking quietly in the parks, her own determined sacrificed to educate herself despite the prejudices against her because of her sex. Her heart went out to them, for she knew how hungrily they thirsted for knowledge. Yet she knew the young women would likely be harassed by the secret police, who saw their desire for education as nothing more than aberrant behaviour. The female students were suspected of all kinds of clandestine activities, simply because they were not at home caring for a father or husband and changing dirty diapers!

Anna had an ear for the tragic story, and couldn't resist the tale told to her by one young woman, who had been born into an aristicratic family. Sent to a convent by her family to keep her out of reach of some undisclosed influences (it may have been a secret lover or a Nihilist or both), the beautiful, dark-eyed girl soon escaped, dressed as a peasant. Anna saw something of herself in the enterprising young woman who would not be locked up in a convent for the rest of her life:

> She then worked her way to Varna as a cabin boy, served a year in a hotel as "boots," when money enough had been saved she purchased suitable clothes and took service as a nursery governess in an English nobleman's family....[22]

But the young girl might have also run away from Russia because of the food. Certainly, Anna had never eaten such uninspired, if not downright revolting, food. She deplored the Russian cuisine, moaning over the great hardship eating had become. She had good reason. Who could stomach cold fish soup with cabbage, beer, cider and salted cucumbers, not to mention fish stewed in rancid butter and vinegar, or greasy hashed veal? Anna found the oatmeal boiled in oil and fermented mare's milk particularly hard to take.

Amidst this culinary nightmare, Anna stumbled on two new ideas which have become quite common in western society. She described to her fascinated readers the curious practise of eating the "roes of certain fish salted," which were called "caviare." This, she wrote, a trifle baffled, was "the most esteemed of national delicacies." Even more curious was a Russian custom which had confounded many a foreigner, easily recognizable in the twentieth century as cocktails and hors d'oeuvres:

> When invited to dinner by a nobleman in Russia, you are ushered into a small room, where stands a tiny table spread with a few dainties, caviare, ham, salt fish, cheese, bread cut in tiny bits, and liqueurs. No chairs are provided, the guests stand around and partake of the various morsels. An Englishman on one occasion astonished his host by disposing of all the dainties spread on the table. When he had finished and was reflecting what a queer dinner he had had, the adjoining door was thrown open and he beheld a magnificent chamber, in which was served a princely dinner in the European style.[23]

Anna might have started a new trend had she brought some of the fine Russian caviar back with her for her editors to sample. They seemed not to notice the oversight.

On her arrival in Boston in mid-1881 she was given a warm reception. In fact, the *Youth's Companion* editorial staff were wildly enthusiastic about the series of articles she had prepared for them. In a letter to her daughter, Anna wrote with great amusement that not only were the editors, Perry Mason and one Mr. Clay, delighted with her articles, but they had offered her a prestigious editorial job on their very popular publication. But it was not to be.

> I felt that if I began to consider the matter I might be tempted to accept the offer in the end. So I said at once and decidedly that my future great work of educating my grandchildren was already begun. There the matter rests for the present.[24]

Her decision made, Anna returned to Halifax with no regrets.

News of her return had already leaked out, and friends, neighbours, and total strangers clamoured for details of her adventure. Soon, Anna had told and re-told her stories so many times that she decided she might as well give a lecture on the subject. It was just what her public wanted. No one seemed to mind paying to see their very own literary lady, considered an exotic addition to the life of the city. Even at that time, Anna received $60 for one of her famously detailed lectures.

Again, word spread fast, and it was scarely even necessary to publicize her talk. On the appointed evening, though, the sky, which had been dark and threatening all day, broke open in a thunderous downpour. Had any other speaker been scheduled the evening would have been a disaster, but for Anna Leonowens, Halifax's social elite gathered in droves beneath the Church of England Institute's gothic spires.[25]

Promptly at 8 o'clock, Anna quietly took the floor. She needed no notes, for every moment of the trip flowed through her head in rich detail and wondrous colour. "Every nation has a hearth," she began, "... a centre where the national heart beats, and from which radiates the deeper sentiments and virtues of the race." The whisperers were soon stifled, and for the next two hours Anna's commanding voice and unbridled eloquence captured every ravishing detail, every sight, sound and very nearly the *smell* of the lives and customs of Russians. The lecture hall was beginning to smell of wet woolens, which steamed a little in chilly air, but the spellbound audience scarcely noticed.

> At the baptism of an infant, which I happened to witness, after the various rites of marching round the font, waving lighted torches, chanting and praying over the child, the priest crosses, with a small camel's hair brush dipped in the chrism; the mouth, the eyes, ears, hands, feet, back and breast of the child, offering up at each touch a singularly beautiful supplication that the eyes may see only what is pure and good, the ears admit no profane sound, that the mouth may be preserved from all unholy conversation, the hands from evil doing, and the little feet from the path of the ungodly.[26]

Every detail of the trip had flowed back to her as she spoke. She saw again the onion domes of St. Basil's Church in Moscow and felt the monotonous rhythm of the steam train as it chugged the hundreds of kilometres across the sweeping Russian steppe. She recalled the night she had lain atop a ceramic stove in a peasant hut. It was the warmest place in the house, and guests considered it an honour to be invited to sleep there.

The applause went far beyond the merely polite; Anna extricated herself as quickly as possible from her admirers, refusing the supper of tea and sandwiches that had been laid out on the excuse that her grandchildren expected a similar story before bedtime. The transfixed *Halifax Morning Herald* reporter was forced to follow her down the stairs and out into Barrington Street, for she would not sit still as he plied her with questions. Anna, who always loved being in the limelight, thoroughly enjoyed the experience.

Anna's literary reputation, launched some 11 years before, continued to grow with the publication of her much-heralded Moscow articles. Her third and fourth books were still to come, but would be based on experiences she had gone over and over in her mind hundreds of times. Although less popular than the first two, *Life and Travel in India* and *Our Asiatic Cousins* reflected a certain maturity of scholarship, an open mindedness and an insatiable curiosity about Eastern countries.

One of her primary influences when she was writing *The English Governess* and *The Romance of the Harem* had been *Uncle*

Tom's Cabin. Its emphasis on Christianity had not been entirely to her own taste, but her publisher, editors and friends had encouraged her to adopt its slightly histrionic style with a view to increasing book sales as well as conforming to accepted Victorian codes of morality. The result was somewhat schizophrenic, but her legions of fans seemed not to notice.

By the time she published *Life and Travel in India*, Anna had developed her own style. Less simplistic and not nearly so moral in tone, the book had given her a chance to display her dazzling talent for detail, an encyclopedic knowledge of Indian customs and language fitted together into an chronology of life under the British Raj; it was, perhaps, less entertaining than what she had written before.

Anna had always been bitterly opposed to the British domination of India. In *Life and Travel in India*, she let those feelings surface again, this time with all the confidence and skill of a master editorial writer:

> The viceroy and the great English grandees are separated from the natives for whose interests they are there by law and custom which nothing can overcome, and the officials around whom the whole Indian empire revolves are often ignorant of the Indian languages, races, religious and social prejudices, and mode of life of the hundreds of provinces that lie within the railways, while those beyond are to them, as the wilds of Africa, an undiscovered country.[27]

It would have taken very little for Anna to be assured forever of a prestigious place in the literary world; she already rubbed shoulders with most of the famous authors of the day. The position she had been offered would have taken her from a writer of exotica, a phenomenon, to that of an established and honoured editorialist. But Anna was ferociously dedicated to her grandchildren, particularly little James, whom she took almost everywhere. Thomas often chided her about filling the boy's head with exotic stories, but it would scarcely do the child any harm to develop a good imagination. In fact, the stories had their effect. As an adult, James joined his uncle Louis in Thailand, working for the Thai government as a medical officer.

The wrangling over the childrens' education went on without either Anna or Thomas thinking to consult Avis, who was, after all, their mother. Had they thought to consult her, Avis would undoubtedly have put in a plea for a little domestic peace; the constant sparring between her husband and her mother grated on her nerves. Besides, she wished James could be allowed some more child-like pursuits that did not involve learning the moral behind every story and hearing a detailed explanation to every problem. Avis could just hear Anna talking in a grave voice to little James, who was barely able to run around, of how

> Life in the East is altogether so novel, so full of dramatic sights and sounds, that one's curiosity seems to grow with the abundant nourishment it finds everywhere. Now one sees a Mohammedan funeral, or the procession of gorgeous Taboots of Moslems, or gods of the Hindoos....[28]

That certainly wasn't the sort of life Avis could ever imagine liking. In fact, she could barely remember her own early days in the Orient. No, Avis was a delicate and shy woman who preferred to spend her days quietly at home with the children, placating the household staff, while her dearly beloved mother was out marshalling a corps of volunteer do-gooders to ever-greater feats of humanitarian and civic accomplishment. Always terribly sensitive, Avis wore herself out in attempting to please not only her husband, but her demanding mother. When the pair united, having made their minds up over something, their will was done. Avis certainly could not screw up her courage to oppose them.[29]

Avis looked out the window of the family's Bishop's Row townhouse, and down over Inglis Street. The problem, she knew, was that her mother and her husband were too much alike. They demanded excellence in everything. Neither ever backed down in an argument, and there were many of them. Yet her husband could be a witty man, and he was well known, down at the bank, for his Fyshe stories. He had laughed long and hard when he read the printed remarks of a colleague, who ventured to call him (from the safety of Chicago) "a Scotchman of cranky disposition but great ability."[30] Avis knew, too, that Thomas was considered to be a fair and kind employer, far ahead of his time in seeking pay raises for his clerks, and even instituting savings and pension plans, virtually unheard-of at the time. Thomas was also courageous. Once, during a drive in Minneapolis, Minnesota,

Thomas saw a young boy drowning in a river. He unhesitatingly jumped into the swirling stream — hat, coat, cigar and all — and saved the youngster's life. He did not stop to receive the congratulations of the assembled crowd, but sensibly hastened back to his hotel for a change of clothes.

At home, it was different. Thomas and Anna had attached such importance to every little thing the children did, or, more significantly, did not do, that Avis often felt as though she had a front row ticket to a melodrama, and was powerless to stop the action. Sometimes, she wondered if her mother felt she was still matching wits with old King Mongkut.

It is no wonder poor Avis felt she had no business interfering in her children's education. After all, her mother had taught kings. Anna's fame as an educator had spread beyond literary circles, and she was frequently called upon to give her opinion of this or that educational system, and to help found a school for boys in New York. Surely, Avis reasoned to herself, if her methods were good enough for royalty, they should be good enough for James, Anna, Avis, and Thomas.

But the heavy-handedness of the elder Anna and Thomas in almost every aspect of the children's lives had a long-lasting effect. The children were subjected to a disciplined homework regime which precluded them playing at their friends' houses. Many years later, Anna Fyshe wrote ruefully,

> We children were of such overwhelming importance that our every deed or misdeed caused them satisfaction or consternation far beyond its merit. Looking back I realize that there was a complete lack of humour in this attitude toward us. The smallest failing was dramatized to dimensions that bordered on tragedy and oftentimes made our dear mother very sad.[31]

Wistfully, she recalled the "two such rare but uncompromising personalities" who maintained a "delicately-balanced relationship" were,

> an extraordinary team, though distinctly strenuous to live with..... Their mutual esteem developed into a rare friendship, strong enough to weather the storms of their ceaseless angry debates and diverging obsessions, in which neither one was ever known to concede even a minor point.

They measured their forces and found each other equal in
strength....[32]

In the Fyshe household, one had to be made of strong stuff
simply to survive the double-barrelled onslaught of Father
Thomas and Grandma Anna. The only peace came when one or
the other, or both, were out of town which. Fortunately, this was
a regular occurrence.

Meeting Royalty

It was 1884. New York's Fifth Avenue Hotel suite was decked out
splendidly, with fresh flowers everywhere. Anna thought she
detected the smell of jasmine in the morning air. When she gave
the cab driver the address, he wanted to know where her luggage
was. It had given her a secret thrill to say she wasn't checking in
herself; she had a special audience with His Royal Highness
Prince Nares of Thailand. The cabbie nearly swallowed his snuff,
and Anna laughed quietly to herself. Some New Yorkers were
impressionable after all.

As she waited on the silk-covered sofa, she fidgeted a bit,
unsure as to just why His Excellency had summoned her. She
wasn't even sure she would recognize him. After all, Anna
hadn't seen him for 17 years. Then, he had been merely the
loveable Prince Krita, son of one of her dearest pupils, Lady Son
Klin, whom she once guided in a rough, but ardent translation of
Uncle Tom's Cabin into Thai.

Now, though, he was the Thai Foreign Minister, a powerful
and trusted ally of King Chulalongkorn here in the United States
on some sort of secret mission for his government. But would he
be upset about her book, *The English Governess at the Siamese
Court*, in which she had said so many things about his father,
King Mongkut? After all, she never had received the bequest the
old king had left her and Louis. Moreover, not only had her book
been banned, but the Thai government had bought up nearly a
whole edition and destroyed it.[33]

Suddenly, the drawing room door burst open and a handsome young man strode toward her. "Mem cha!" he exclaimed,
clasping his hands around her neck just as he had done when he
was a little boy. It was as if time had stood still. He was much
older, of course, but the prince had retained his boyish enthusiasm and unfettered honesty. She needn't have worried
what the prince thought about her book; he never mentioned it.

In fact, the king had specifically asked him to do everything he could to see his former governess while he was in New York.

That the king had thought enough of Anna to insist his minister contact her and pass along his good wishes wasn't all that astounding. Louis, still in Thailand, was in Chulalongkorn's thoughts frequently. The strapping young man had initially landed himself a plum position in the king's army, where he was put to work defending the monarch from intrigue and the royal lands from marauding tribesmen. In reality, Louis had spent much of his time trooping around the remote provinces, as far away from the intrigues and bureaucracy of the Court as possible.

Louis soon earned a reputation as a wild character and was more than occasionally enmeshed in financial and emotional scandals. He was held in high esteem by the Thais, however, and seemed to have inherited his mother's charitable instincts. A few years later, King Chulalongkorn granted him a concession to harvest teak in the northern provinces. He already knew the territory well from his soldierly excursions, and became wealthy from logging Thai teak.[34]

Anna and the prince talked for well over an hour about Louis, Chulalongkorn and other former pupils. In particular, Anna was eager for news of one of her most studious and fervent disciples, Lady Son Klin. Prince Nares was glad to give it, for he had instantly recognized the uncut emerald ring his mother had given Anna so many years before. "Mem," he said suddenly, "if you want any money at any time you must let His Majesty know, for he says that all that he ever learned of good in his life you taught him."[35]

Later that evening, at the suggestion of Anna's old friend, Mr. Paine, a lavish reception was held in the hotel for the prince. Not only did the aging and slightly eccentric magnate delightedly act as host, he paid for everything from the champagne to the paper-thin slices of roast beef. The only reward he wanted was to meet Prince Nares. Anna had described the prince again and again to the old man and he had never tired of the tale. "I am very glad to meet you," he thundered at the slight prince, giving him a hearty handshake. "I always thought you were a myth but now I see you are a reality."

Anna and the prince were the centre of attention; the prince would begin a sentence in Thai, and Anna would finish it for him, to the delight of the assembled guests. The gathering lasted well into the night, but Anna, ever the disciplined writer, sat down immediately to compose a triumphant letter to Avis back in Halifax detailing the day's extraordinary events. The best news of all was that there had been dramatic changes in Thailand during her absense. The prince had told her during their private meeting, much to her delight, that if she went back to Thailand now,

> ... I would hardly know the place, or the people, so changed were they in almost every respect: prostration, slavery, imprisonment of wife or child for the husband or father's debts were all abolished; that new roads and canals were built, schools endowed wherein all European and Oriental instruction was taught....He also added that this was the result of my teaching the present King and the royal family....[36]

Here, at last, was Anna's vindication for all of the battles, and all of the years she had fought against what she had truly believed in her heart was an unfair system. The thoughtful seeds she had so carefully cultivated so many years before in the gardens of her young pupils' minds had at last flowered and borne fruit.

Endnotes

1. Landon, Margaret, *op.cit.*, p. 363.
2. This actually had quite the opposite effect.
3. Leonowens, Anna. *The English Governess, op.cit.*, preface.
4. Bristowe, W.S., *Louis and the King of Siam*, Chatto & Windus, 1976, p.36.
5. Landon, Margaret, *op.cit.*, p. 369.
6. Bristowe, *op.cit.*, pp. 36-7.
7. Thomas Fyshe would go on to become one of Canada's most successful bankers.
8. Forman's Division, in south-end Halifax, is named for him. His property ran from Young Ave. to MacLean St. Subsequently, it became Thorndean, the home J.S. MacLean, elected president of the BNS in 1874.
9. The personals column of the *Halifax Morning Herald* noted the departure of "Mr. Thomas Fyshe and lady" from Quebec City to Liverpool, aboard the RMS *Circassian* on June 29th.
10. Avis and Thomas had six children: James Carlyle, born the year after their marriage, 1879; Anna Harriet Leonowens (1881 or 1882); Thomas

Maxwell (1883); Avis Selina (1886); Kathleen (?); and Frank (?); they also raised George and Anna Harriet Leonowens, Louis's children.

11. This excerpt was taken from *Readings from the Best Authors*, part of the Nova Scotia School Series, published in Halifax by A. & W. MacKinlay & Co., 1865, p. 47.

12. *Saturday Night*, vol. 21, April 21, 1888, p. 6.

13. *Ibid.*

14. Raddall, Thomas. *Halifax, Warden of the North*, McClelland & Stewart (Toronto, 1974), p. 193. On October 4, 1962, *The Mail Star* reported 13 per cent of boys living at Africville under age 10 went to work while only one per cent of the other population of Halifax boys (i.e., white) in this age group did likewise. A need for improved education was recommended, as well as better housing and jobs for black who were considered second class citizens.

15. General information taken from *The Dark Side of Life in Victorian Halifax* by Judith Fingard, Pottersfield Press (Halifax, 1989).

16. Anna's descriptions of her trip remain as fresh and evocative today as they were at the time.

17. The Nihilist movement began in Russia around 1860 and advocated the destruction of existing social, political and economic institutions. They tried to achieve their aims with terrorism and assassination.

18. Leonowens, A. H. "Moscow, 'The Holy'" in *The Critic*, New York, June, 1887, no. 2.

19. Fyshe, Anna Harriet Leonowens. "Anna: From the unpublished memoirs of Anna Harriet Leonowens Fyshe," in *Chatelaine*, Jan., 1962, pp. 60-64.

20. *The Critic, op.cit.*

21. *Ibid.*

22. *Ibid.*

23. *Ibid.*

24. Letter from Anna Leonowens to her daughter Avis, dated 1881. From *Chatelaine, op.cit.*, p. 64.

25. This graceful and unique building continues to enliven Halifax's downtown district under the somewhat ignominious but popular name, The Bean Sprout Building.

26. *The Critic, op.cit.*

27. Leonowens, Anna Harriette. *Life and Travel in India: Being recollections of a journey before the days of railroads*, Porter & Coates (Philadelphia, 1884), p. 321.

28. *Life and Travel in India, op.cit.*, p. 65.

29. Schull Joseph and Douglas J. Gibson. *The Scotiabank Story*, MacMillan of Canada (Toronto, 1982). It is noted in this official history of the Bank of Nova Scotia that Thomas Fyshe's letters "...indicate the mutual admiration and respect that Fyshe and his famous mother-in-law had for each other," p. 52.

30. *The Scotiabank Story, op.cit.*, p. 52.
31. *Chatelaine, op.cit.*
32. *Chatelaine, op.cit.*
33. *The English Governess at the Siamese Court* is still unavailable in Thailand.
34. The Louis T. Leonowens Company still operates in Thailand, with offices in Bangkok.
35. Landon, Margaret, *op.cit.*, p. 371.
36. *Ibid.*, p. 371.

Barrington Street East, Halifax, circa 1880, showing the Church
of England Institute (now known as the Bean Sprout Building)
where Anna Leonowens lectured. (Public Archives of Nova
Scotia.

A stern Thomas Fyshe, shown in early middle age. Notman photograph.

The Union Bank of Canada on Hollis Street , Halifax, the
first home of the Victoria School of Art. (Public Archives
of Nova Scotia)

Granville Street East, Halifax, circa 1880, where the Anna
Leonowens Gallery is now located. It is the only institution in
Canada that bears her name. (Public Archives of Nova Scotia)

Chapter Four

A Lasting Impression
1887-1897

There are hundreds less worthy of the title than Mrs. Leonowens who have taken rank among the benefactors of mankind.

from Boston Transcript, as quoted in the
Halifax Herald, June 19, 1897

Anna hurried down Pleasant Street past the sprawling charm of Government House, ignoring the comfort of a cup of tea with Mrs. Malachy Daly, the lieutenant-governor's capable wife. Her nerves were frazzled and her heart heavier than it had been since the death of Leon nearly forty years before. The front door of number 235 slammed behind her rather too sharply; the startled Mary MacQuarrie, who had come out to receive her mistress's mantle and hat, went away empty handed. Anna went straight to the morning room and shut the door behind her.

She slumped exhausted in front of her desk, the weight of six decades of resilience collapsing. Anna stared at the carriages clipping smartly along the street outside as the mantle clock ticked off minute after minute. Then taking a fresh sheet of paper and filling her pen, she poured out her grief:

> The Board of Directors of the Victoria School of Art and Design met this morning to perform one of the most painful duties which has devolved upon its members since its inception, i.e., to express their deep sorrow personally and publicly and to deplore the death of one of their most-cherished and gifted members, the late Mrs. J. F. Kenny and above all to place on record their high appreciation of the nobility of her character; while giving expression to their profound sympathy with her husband Mr. J. F. Kenny and entire household who have lost a member of such rare excellence of character, and such varied accomplishments and graces.[1]

Here the precision of her penmanship wavered; she could not help a tear or two dropping onto the paper. Helen Kenny, her dear friend and colleague, once voted the most beautiful woman in Halifax by her admirers, was dead. The woman whose organizational capabilities were second only to her own, and whose charm and beauty were legend, would never again enliven Anna's Monday afternoon at-homes with her lively wit. Helen Kenny would never again march with her to the Mayor's office, tempering Anna's brusque intellect with her own brand of influence and charm to gain this or that improvement, favour or concession. Taking a deep breath, Anna continued her moving testament to the woman who had become almost as dear as her own daughter:

> It has been exceedingly gratifying and duly characteristic, to find that Mrs. Kenny's interest in the school continued unabated to the very last weeks almost of her life.

But in her vibrant friend's untimely death, Anna saw a glimmer of hope. Helen had wanted a permanent home for the art college as badly as Anna, and had worked tirelessly using her considerable connections to try to wrest a building, or even a building site from the municipal, provincial, and eventually Dominion officials, so that the art college could finally be firmly established in the fabric of the city's cultural life. But the dream went farther: Anna foresaw not just a building but an ambitious arts complex that would house the provincial museum, a hodgepodge of city libraries, overflow from the Legislative Library, as well as various scientific and cultural associations.

So far, the combined efforts of some of the most influential women in Halifax, and by proxy, their husbands, had been to no avail. Dr. Honeyman, curator of the Institute of Natural Science, or whatever one might call his overflowing collection of bones and fossils and relics, was a strong supporter. Then there was the petition in favour of the complex, signed by hundreds. Anna had been very satisfied to see the names of Helen's husband, and her own Thomas Fyshe near the top of the list. And, until his death in 1887, she had been able to count on Sir William Young (the former Premier, and later the Chief Justice of Nova Scotia) to urge consolidation of the various reading rooms and library collections. So it seemed the time was at last ripe for this great, progressive vision to come to pass in the form a building that would house the Victoria School of Art and Design and commemorate Halifax's most vibrant hostess.

However, Anna's heartfelt appeal that Helen's death wish be granted was not to be fulfilled yet. The arts and museum complex, Anna's most forward-looking dream, would never come to pass.

She sighed, and smoothed the folds of her grey silk dress. It had all seemed so much simpler that June day in 1887 when she had sat in the Orpheus Hall at the triumphant first annual meeting. She tried to dismiss the feeling of intense satisfaction that swept over her at seeing her name at the top of the list of nominees for the Board of Directors. It was on that board, and as a college vice-president that her alliance with Helen had first been forged.

There was also, of course, the powerful alliance of Dr. Eliza Ritchie, the first woman professor of Dalhousie College, and her sister, Mary. These determined daughters of the province's current chief justice were undaunted by most obstacles in their paths, and not at all concerned that their activities were looked on with some scepticism by the public.

Then, for the first time that sad day, Anna smiled a little. She had been thinking of her very first drawing school, which had begun as an impromptu tutorial for the precocious and talented Princess Fa-Ying, the favourite child of King Mongkut. The petted eight-year-old had sat beside her one hot Bangkok day long ago, happily drawing the morning away, an activity she eminently preferred to Sanskrit class. This child, like her many brothers and sisters, was imbued with a natural sense of artistry, enhanced by the breathtaking beauty of the many gilded temples and palaces that was her heritage.

Perhaps that child's enthusiasm for drawing had inspired her to found the Victoria School of Art and Design[2]. Anna smiled again at the thought of the Fa-Ying's youthful spirit springing to life again in some incomprehensible Buddhist fashion to enliven and enlighten its hallways and classrooms. Many members of Halifax's middle- and upper-class families sketched, particularly women. But the children of the mean streets of Halifax, the labourers, the tradesmen and the draughtsmen, had no knowledge of aesthetics, little inclination, and almost no means of obtaining such training.

It was toward these people Anna's real efforts were directed. She had no real wish to form a club that would turn ladies into artists. Rather, she hoped formal education would bring "a higher artistic value to all the various branches of mechanical and industrial arts"[3] for the young men and women of Halifax.

Anna hadn't resorted to the Thai custom of consulting astrologers to determine when the time was ripe to launch her ambitious college, but had seemingly happened upon it anyway, for things moved quickly in that founding year. Known as "one of the cleverest women who ever occupied the lecture platform,"[4] Anna put her own talents to use, raising $60 from a lecture in Charlottetown, Prince Edward Island. And then there was the fortuitous success of the World's Fayre[sic]. The whole thing hadn't been exactly to her taste, but Helen, with her infallible sense of what the Halifax citizenry considered good fun, had put her stamp on the event.

The slightly unconventional but wildly successful fundraiser lasted a whole week that August of 1888. The Exhibition Hall was packed with a throng of 10,000 and raised an almost unthinkable $5,000 for the school building fund. Helen had indeed lived up to her reputation as "one of the chief leaders of gaiety of Halifax." At least that was the opinion of an obviously smitten *Mercury* reporter, who had gushed over Helen Kenny's "dark beauty," beautiful figure and face, and had not failed to observe that "her dark eyes are the subject of many a toast."[5] In its inaugural year, the school also put on a lavish ball to commemorate Queen Victoria's Golden Jubilee. It was held on Midsummer's Eve (perhaps another suggestion of Helen's, with her romantic notions); Halifax society had turned out in force to whirl around the floor of the Exhibition Hall, under electric light, no less, until the wee hours of the morning.

Anna was still lost in her reverie when Mary came in with a lunch tray. She had ignored the dinner bell, the noise of the children scrambling to the table, and even the hushed whispers outside the door. She looked at the tray absently as the street railway tram rumbled by, rattling the dainty china. She had no interest in the food; her thoughts were still far away. She sighed again, and couldn't help but feel a little overwhelmed at how much there was still to do.

In 1888, Anna had masterminded the overseas educational sojourn of the Fyshe family, but events earlier in the year very nearly conspired to prevent her departure. For one thing, the art school was barely on its feet, and badly needed her firm and inspired direction. For another thing, she had just put the final touches on her fourth book, *Our Asiatic Cousins*, and had made arrangements for it to be published the following year by D. Lothrop Co. of Boston.

The very title of this latest, and last, of Anna's books was a little shocking, for it was an era when Orientals were specifically denied the vote in Canada, and when even the progressive and determined Lady Aberdeen confided to her diary that, "it is difficult to feel towards a Chinaman as a real human being."[6]

Perhaps she was willing to gamble some of her prestige to throw new light on an area that was the subject of much prejudice and superstition. Certainly, she seemed to have had an ally in the *Halifax Herald*, at least regarding Confucius: "Mrs. Leonowens has made very lifelike and human this great preacher who for nearly twenty-four centuries has received the adoration of his countrymen."[7]

Anna never equalled the success of her first two books with their fantastic tales of wealth and corruption, slavery and injustice, but she had demonstrated her uncanny acumen for the kind of socio-anthropological writing that her more astute readers had come to expect. Nor had *Life and Travel in India*, published in 1884, been the bestseller she had hoped. In concentrating on ravishingly detailed accounts of life and social custom, downplaying tyranny and repression, she subverted her own righteous influence which, more than anything else, had been the successful formula of *The English Governess*.

In effect, Anna may have sacrificed some of her share of the popular market in favour of the truth. Although she still wrote from the more popularly engaging perspective of a wide-eyed young woman, she in fact had a vast knowledge of her subjects. After all, she was an Oriental scholar, conversant in 11 languages (and probably more if she stopped to count them all).[8] She had long outgrown the creative confines of the merely sensational popular novel which so often struck a balance between Christian uprightness, moral indignation and propriety, particularly when the topic at hand was a so-called heathen culture.

A third, more sensational event, also threatened to play havoc with her intended departure for Europe. Anna had left Halifax on December 7 with 10-year-old James, bound for New York. She had intended a leisurely Christmas visit to call on old friends there and in Boston. But things didn't work out quite as planned.

A few days after their arrival in New York City, Anna became embroiled in a sensational law suit centering around John Paine, who had died three years before. She had been a little put off to see her friend and benefactor described in the newspapers as a "rich miser."

The trial commenced on January 24, 1888 before a packed courtroom. Many of the spectators were strangers who had come just to see what it was that all of New York was talking about. They might just as well have stayed home, for the press carried detailed daily descriptions of the suit launched by William Paine, his grandson, who charged that his inheritance had been squandered before he'd even had a chance to claim it.

During the years Anna had lived with Avis on Staten Island, she had become a close friend of John Paine, a rich and slightly eccentric entrepreneur. The old man had died in 1885 at age 91. Anna, who had last seen her friend in 1884, had been called to testify about his mental stability, a crucial element that would determine the validity of numerous property transfers made before his demise.

Mr. Paine's will stipulated that his enormous wealth, including several palatial homes and prime New York land, be divided between William Paine and his daughter-in-law, Virginia Paine. His second wife was to receive $6,000 per year for the rest of her life. But before he died, Mr. Paine deeded his wife and nieces a fortune in New York City property. Yet when it came time to settle his estate, the remaining real estate was found to be worth only $23,000. The effectively disinherited grandson claimed his old and feeble grandfather had been swindled; the defence claimed otherwise.

Testifying for the defence, the "well-known literary lady," as she was described by the *New York Times*, said when she last saw Mr. Paine, his mind was as sharp as ever.

> Once he told her that he lamented bitterly being rich, and said she was unfortunate in being poor.... He told her he liked her lectures because they came to an end.[9]

Gazing down at the sumptuous emerald ring Lady Son Klin had given her, Anna said she had never had any business transactions with Mr. Paine, despite the fact that she must have met him at a time when she was in dire need of money.

98

Anna proved an exceptionally deft witness — for herself. After giving the court extensive background on herself, her books and her travels (this was a masterful bit of public relations, since she undoubtedly knew her testimony would be reported in some detail in the daily newspapers), Anna nonetheless managed to confirm Mr. Paine's presence of mind when he had quipped to her friend, Prince Krita that he "always thought you were a myth; now I can see you are a reality." Coincidentally, the story also served to reinforce her own impeccable connections with royalty. The *New York Times* covered the case in detail, particularly Anna's interesting testimony.

The sensational trial lasted eight days, and wound up with the jury unable to make a decision. A new trial would have to be held. The nasty business had already kept Anna so long in New York she began to worry that she would not have time to tie up all the loose ends of her life before the family sailed away without her on the steam packet for London. She fled back to Halifax the next day, and such a flurry of packing and organizing and cleaning and sweeping Bishop's Row had never seen. At the end of March, the family sailed for London.

Although most of the work of shutting up the house was done, a slightly bewildered Thomas Fyshe was left to make his own arrangements for accommodation. In the end, having dithered over whether to take a flat, he landed at the Waverley Hotel on Pleasant Street,[10] a genteel establishment where a man like himself might feel comfortable. Harder to endure than the lack of familiar and domestic comforts was the separation from his wife and children. Perhaps he even felt a pang or two whenever he recalled a particularly inspired bout of verbal combat with his voluble mother-in-law. It was not an experience Thomas had looked forward to, although he had doubtless put on a brave face before his family.

The truth was, the normally stalwart Scot missed them even before they had gone, and confided his feelings in a letter to a friend on March 28, 1888:

> I begin to feel a little queer at the prospect of losing my whole family for an indefinite period. I hope it is for the best, but one needs some self-reliance to do what nobody else does and what most people seem to condemn. I shall feel better a fortnight hence if they get over all right and get snugly settled down in Deutschland.[11]

By May 14, Thomas wasn't any happier, but he seemed relieved that his family had arrived safely in Cassel, a town in northern Germany. To Mr. Greaves, a friend of Anna's from Boston, he wrote that his family liked their adopted land "very much and the children seem to be thriving. I suppose they are all speaking German by this time. I am consequently leading a very lonely life, but I seem to stand it very well."[12]

Indeed, Thomas seems to have willingly made the sacrifice in order that his children would have the best education possible. But when his family returned after five years abroad, he found himself in the odd position of having two more children to raise.

Death of a Royal Daughter

Louis Leonowens had been foraging around in the remote hills of Chiang Mai for some time when he heard his beloved wife, the daughter of a Thai princess, had only a few weeks to live. The frantic Louis arrived in Bangkok in less than two weeks. It was a Herculean achievement considering the remoteness and roughness of the terrain. He was at her bedside when she died of kidney disease at age 36.[13] The same ailment would paralyse, and later kill, his friend King Chulalongkorn.

Louis's first thoughts were for the future of his children, a son, George, and yet another Anna Harriet. With surprising swiftness, he arranged to bring them to London, where Anna was temporarily residing. She had never met them and, in fact, hadn't seen her son for 20 years, but agreed, wholeheartedly, to bring up the two children.

Louis and family arrived in September, and immediately took up residence at the Waterloo Hotel in London. Anna marvelled at how the freewheeling Louis had changed since she had last seen him. Although still the eager, impatient boy always restless for something new, he was obviously chastened by the sudden death of his beloved and gentle wife.[14] Underneath, though, Anna detected an element of self-discipline her son, now 38, had not possessed as a young man. Moreover, he had gained some business acumen. She had to admit that success agreed with him, even if his lavish lifestyle was not entirely to her taste. If the truth be known, Louis had very nearly achieved the fairy-tale life he had dreamed about as a youngster in the king's palace, first in the King's service and then in the country's lucrative teak forests. In a word, he was "loaded."[15]

The unwieldy entourage, consisting of the six Fyshe children, Anna and Avis, plus the opulently dressed Louis and his two children, their nurse Lena, and Louis's manservant Pang, retreated to Margate.

The seaside holiday was brief, but it was enough for Louis to recover his equilibrium. Shortly afterwards, he returned to superintend his thriving business in Thailand. In the ensuing years, he led a rather wild life in the teak forests, keeping several common-law wives and a harem. Perhaps Anna sympathized with her son in his grief, recalling the tragedy of her own husband's death. If she found out about his rowdy behaviour, she kept it to herself.

The two newest, if slightly bewildered, members of the clan were welcomed vigorously into the fold. Thomas Fyshe likely made many jokes about his wife being away for five years and bringing him back two more children to raise. In fact, Thomas was relieved simply to renounce his lonely life as a bachelor banker and resume his role as patriarch.

Instead of departing for Europe in 1888 to supervise her grandchildren's schooling, Anna might have been wiser to stay home and tend the flickering flame of the new art college. The school was barely established on an upper floor of the Union Bank Building, and then thanks only to the influence of Thomas Fyshe (manager of the Bank of Nova Scotia down the street) who had had a word with the proper authorities. She remained abroad for five long years, devoting herself to the one task she always gave precedence: supervising the education of her grandchildren. In her absence, the efforts of the Board, including the valiant Helen, had not been enough to put the college smoothly and forever on the road to success, and it had soon faltered. And what a mess had awaited Anna on her return.

As early as 1889, a fatalistic atmosphere had descended over the art school directors, who searched feebly for a silver lining in a cloudy future: "Although the attendance for the ensuing year does not promise to be very large, yet it is felt that it represents as much genuine artistic ability as the unnaturally large and unduly stimulated attendance of the past and hence forward there will be as the product of the school itself a yearly growing constituency to improve and perpetuate its good work for the community."

Subsequent meetings didn't produce a much more optimistic outlook. The annual meeting scheduled for Sept. 30, 1890 was adjourned for a month until someone could collect the school fees. When they resumed October 28, it was found the treasurer was out of town. On November 11, they tried again, but the school fees were still uncollected and even board members had to be urged to pay their dues and subscriptions! The following year's meeting didn't fare any better. Scheduled for September 18, 1891, it was cancelled for lack of a quorum.[16]

It was not until Anna's return that the dismal situation was taken in hand. On September 29, 1893, as she gazed sternly over the assembled membership, her unspoken disapproval fairly thundered off the walls of the mayor's office. Even the auditor trembled a little as he gave his report, all the more so because he had nothing to report. He had not been able to check the receipts of fees collected because no one had troubled themselves to give him access to the records!

It was the last straw. Anna had not felt so frustrated since her days dealing with the bumbling Siamese bureaucracy. There was nothing left to do but to apply the same principles which had worked so successfully there. She would simply take charge. Anna moved quickly, and before the meeting was over, had organized the board once again into some semblance of order. With Mrs. Kenny seconding her, she had a committee appointed to look after obtaining a city grant. The two confederates were its sole members. A building committee was also struck, with Helen as Anna's trusty lieutenant. Teachers, it was commanded, would henceforth keep a class book with attendance and fees paid duly noted.

But the new management was not enough to retain the services of the long-suffering head master, George Harvey; he was replaced in 1893 by Ozias Dodge of the Art Students League in New York. But Dodge lasted only a year and was succeeded by Charles Waterbury. Within the year, Waterbury suffered a serious illness, and by the time classes opened for the 1895-96 school term, the school had its first female head. Catherine Evans was appointed, largely on Anna's recommendation, despite mutterings that a woman was not capable of holding the office.

There was still the matter of permanent premises to contend with. Anna bluntly told anyone who would listen (and she hoped the mayor was one of them) that "the school opened with 125 pupils. But owing to the fact that the present accommodation is totally inadequate to the needs of the community [the registrars] have been obliged, much to their regret, to refuse quite a number of applicants for the night classes which are at present overcrowded."[17]

Anna was now playing by Bangkok rules. She had little to lose, since it seemed her school was going down the drain anyway. She put aside any thoughts she may have had for propriety, and drew the sharp sword of elocution in her own defence. The object of her wrath was none other than Premier William Stevens Fielding, who had dared to double-cross her. In a long-winded complaint to the Halifax Local Council of Women in 1896, Anna made no bones about what she had decided must have been adept political manipulation at her expense, or at the very least, some smooth words designed to placate and patronize her:

> The Premier received the delegation, as is his wont, most kindly, gave them every encouragement to hope they would find ample accommodation in the proposed building, on the payment of course of an adequate rent for the art school students. But nearly a year has passed since and nothing decisive has been heard of the proposed new building, or a free site where they could put up a public building with sufficient accommodation...."[18]

She did not fail to note that the constant demand for skilled draughtsmen in the city had been partly created by the school itself. "This is one of the many instances in which the ordinary principles of commercial life is reversed." Anna chastised humanity in general as "the only animal whose desires increase as they are supplied, he is the only creature who is never satisfied."

> All other living creatures crave nothing more than they did thousands of years ago. But it is not so with man. No sooner are his animal wants satisfied, than an indefinable something urges him forward, onward, upward; man has set his feet on the first step of an infinite progression; and it ought to be the great aim of teachers and legislators to help him on this path of progression. Therefore it is that in regard to all the material wants of our kind, to all that has become familiar and traditional it is demand that creates a supply.[19]

Anna continued to fight for a permanent home for her beloved art school until she left the city in 1897, but it wasn't until long after her involvement with the institution had ceased that her dream was realized.[20]

But for Anna, the dream came true too late. She never saw the Victoria School of Art and Design's new home, at the corner of Argyle and George Streets for by then, Anna was living in Montreal, and tragedy had again struck her life. Her daughter, Avis, had died the year before of food poisoning at age 47, and Anna was in mourning. The tragic accident left the elderly Anna in the unwelcome position of housebound mother to eight boisterous young people.

Whether out of grief, illness, or her new wifely duties, Anna no longer had the inclination to leave Montreal. She had not, however, lost any of her old *sang froid*. With the customary stuffiness she reserved for formal correspondence, Anna wrote (using the third person) a note dated March 28, 1903 in which she quite honestly observed that "nothing would have given her greater pleasure than to have been present among her old friends on such an auspicious occasion."

As the ceremony marking the opening of the college's first permanent home arrived, Anna felt little joy. The great day for which she had worked so hard had been overshadowed by the personal tragedies which had begun to well up around her.

The Local Council of Women

> ...Buddha asked her what she had done with her baby, and she answered that she had buried him and that her heart was sick for all those who had suffered as she had. Then Buddha said, 'Sister, you have found the mustard seed.' That is the little grain that became the first council of Women. She went and taught other women how to tend their babies. She told her husband, 'Our child is dead, but I am going to teach myself so that if I should have another child I can train him.'
>
> Anna Leonowens[21]

Dr. Maria Angwin tossed back her short, unfashionably bobbed hair and laughed heartily at the pantomime before her. Mrs. Leonowens was reciting, in graphic and humorous detail, how she and Mrs. Daly had marched, two by two, straight into the mayor's office and demanded a separate prison cell. To hear

Anna tell it, the incredulous and flustered mayor seemed to think the two ladies wanted to occupy it themselves. His Worship was so relieved when they explained that the cell was necessary to separate neophyte women prisoners from their more hardened female brethren that he agreed to the plan at once.

Securing better prison accommodation for incarcerated women was a pet project of Dr. Angwin, who, as the first and, at the moment, sole woman doctor in Halifax, was often called to the Halifax Police Station to tend the unfortunate captives within. Often, there was not much she could do for those lodged in the dismal and dank edifice. Tuberculosis was rampant; diphtheria and typhoid were common. From time to time, even cholera raised its fearful head, often carried into port by the merchant marine or on ships overloaded with immigrants.

The matter of segregation of women prisoners was first raised at the Local Council of Women's first annual meeting one chilly December day in 1894. At the group's next meeting a month later in Mrs. Daly's charming Government House drawing room, they reported success. A partitioned room would be established for first-time offenders as well as what was referred to as the better class of women who found themselves behind bars. To their bitter disappointment, however, the ladies learned once again that a promise and an action were two different things. Despite his good intentions, His Worship still had not created the cell in question by the following January (a whole year later). On a fierce follow-up visit from the same deputation, he pledged to have the Chief of Police look to the matter immediately. This time, the Mayor was as good as his word. He reported to Anna's deputation that there had been some progress: a wooden floor had been put down in the ordinary cells for women, a tremendous improvement over the rough and cold stone floor. In an excessive display of philanthropic spirit, he also told them he had ordered flooring put down in the men's cells, plus a bed behind a partition for any sick prisoner. "On the whole," Anna told the February, 1896 meeting of the Halifax Local Council of Women, "this committee feels it has done good work."

Dr. Angwin had found another crusade. Even her male colleagues were hesitant to walk some of the streets where Dr. Angwin went out alone, often late at night, with only a hat pin for self-defense. She never refused anyone who asked for her assistance, even if it came from the sorry and neglected houses on Albermarle Street below the Citadel or another impoverished neighbourhood. What Dr. Angwin saw there upset her greatly. She was particularly worried about the number of young children, many no more than toddlers, hanging about the street at 9 and even 10 p.m., some of them smoking, and all of them dirty.

"These children are prey for the hunters of human souls," she told the Council. "Every child has the right to be well born, in the sense of being born well and after that to be well cared for."[22] The result of her convincing argument was a resolution introduced at the Council's second annual meeting that a 9 p.m. curfew be imposed on children under 16, unless accompanied by a parent or guardian.

Anna, ever the civil libertarian, thought the measure rather Draconian, and was about to point out the unfortunate repercussions the Council might feel as a result, when Miss Mabel Parsons piped up: "So much harm can be done between the hours of eight and nine," she contended, that the curfew, in fact, ought to be eight o'clock.

Anna could hold her tongue no longer:

> I would beg to say that, owing to the condition of things here, we have to proceed very carefully. It would seem a breach of the Habeas Corpus Act to infringe upon the freedom of our citizens, and hence, in bringing this legislative measure forward by the Women's Local Council we have to be very careful not to get the entire city, in fact the whole province, set against us as being officious and overdoing things. This ought to be put in such a form that the parents be first approached with regard to the matter and if parents are found not amenable to the law, then those children who have no responsible parents or guardians, and who have not an idea of right and wrong, should be seen after.

For good measure, she repeated a conversation she had heard between two young female factory workers who vehemently opposed the council's proposed curfew. The young women worked 12 hours daily. Because of their youth, an 8 p.m. or even a 9 p.m. curfew would severely limit their shopping and socializing hours. Clearly, Anna felt, this was a case where the council had to think out a more logical solution to the problem.

Anna made it clear she felt the issue of children on the streets late at night should be dealt with in a less authoritarian way. In fact, she was more concerned about the pressing problem of truancy. Truancy, although rampant, was largely ignored by school and municipal officials, partially because of the severe punishments that the offence could draw. (In Halifax alone, 2,000 children out of 7,500 did not attend school, even for the minimum 120 days required out of the 200-day school year.) Despite her desire for change, Anna again recommended caution, taking care to point out that in most cases the punishment for these young offenders was worse than the crime. Truant children were normally incarcerated behind the grim walls of the Industrial School or in St. Patrick's Home for criminal children, and Anna knew that any child thus educated could expect only the grimmest of futures.

> I think it is simply this, that no child who is simply truant from school should be subjected to any influence but the highest and that he could not possibly find in a mixed reformatory school.

That neither Anna nor any of her female colleagues had the right to implement the reforms they discussed was a source of endless frustration. But to Anna, their right to do so was perfectly logical and justified:

> Ladies, all we have to say is, that as our children go to school, and as the girls as well as boys go to school there should therefore be women on the school board and I am quite sure that every mother, when her daughter is at school, has often occasions when she would very much like to be there to modify or make more severe the rules in regard to her children.

Inspired by Anna's logic, the Council moved that in light of

> ...the direct and vital interest which the women of these provinces have in the public schools in which children are being educated, women should be able to be school trustees or members of public school board and philanthropic institutions funded by governments.[23]

Thus, it was Anna who often led the charge for reform, having taken her role as a Victorian matriarch to heart with a formidable conviction matched by a whirlwind of activity. It was not without just cause that *The Chronicle* called her "one of the busiest women in the city...never too busy to render assistance in every good work." The efforts of Anna and her colleagues were vital in a garrison town, plagued by crime and corruption, violence and villainy.

Having grown up in a military family stationed in another far-flung British outpost, Anna knew only too well the economic misery of those left behind. Her heart went out to the women and children left in such desperate poverty in the miserable houses along Albermarle and Barrack streets. Even more distressing was the desperate plight of the city's black residents, condemned for the most part to a life of drudgery as servants and labourers, marginalized in their own corner of the city.

Armed with a copy of Harriet Beecher Stowe's wildly popular book, Anna had for years championed civil rights for all and decried the evils of slavery to anyone who would listen. Now, she wondered if there wasn't something just as important as freedom. As Dr. Angwin had so wisely pointed out, every child, and indeed everyone, had the right to be born well, and to be well-cared for.

Sisterhood

> Ladies Musical Club decided to play bridge and had several grand slams!
>
> *The Evening Chronicle*[24]

Thomas Fyshe chuckled to himself, and tucked the evening paper under his arm before entering the house. Just visible below his elbow was an item he was confident would rile Mrs. Leonowens considerably. It was a report of an unfortunate mishap which had befallen members of the Ladies Musical Club earlier that day, the details of which were rather gleefully described.

The ladies had been going about their business doing good works, in this case arranging the Schubert Memorial Concert to raise money for the Indian famine fund. The concert had been scheduled for that evening, and would mark the debut of the Halifax Symphony Orchestra. The arrangements had been proceeding smoothly until, urged on by Miss Kate Mackintosh, organist of the Brunswick St. Church and founder of the Musical Club, the good ladies had attempted to raise the excessively heavy and unwieldy lid of the grand piano. While they were thus occupied, the piano slid by degrees along the stage, and finally right over the edge, taking several of the ladies with it. The whole embarrassing incident had wound up with a slightly bruised Rose Nevill picking up a piano leg from the twisted wreckage and brandishing it in fury at the hapless Kate.

Thomas had been right. Anna was indeed distinctly displeased when she heard. Her sour mood pervaded the house for a week as the children scrambled to keep up with the extra homework she had assigned to appease her wrath. The incident had come unpleasantly to Anna's mind again that noon hour, as she put the final touches on a speech she would give that afternoon to the Dominion Enfranchisement Association. The grand slam had become a running joke in Halifax, but what was to happen shortly afterwards was no laughing matter.

Support for suffrage was seriously on the wane. The last of a series of motions to give voting rights to women was introduced in the Nova Scotia legislature in 1897. It was defeated by a resounding 26 to 6 vote. It would be 19 years before another suffrage vote was introduced in Province House. The loudly-trumpeted opinion of the Hon. J. W. Longley didn't help either. He took every opportunity to insist that voting would interfere with women's true vocation

> ...first the bearing and bringing up of children, and this is the highest. Second, the creating of home and the beautifying of life...Third, to charm men and make the world pleasant, sweet and agreeable to live in. Fourth, to be kindly and loving, to be sweet and to be cherished, to be weak and confiding, to be protected and to be the object of man's devotion.[25]

The very thought of his deliberately demeaning speech infuriated her. From then on, she had made it a point of principle to convince all and sundry of the essentiality of giving the franchise for women.

With Longley's patronizing words still ringing in her ears, she abruptly took her hat and mantle from the front hall closet and stepped out into Pleasant Street, glad for the ten-minute walk downtown. She would speak directly after May Wright Sewall, the pioneering leader of a lively suffrage movement in the United States. The legislative assembly chamber of Province House would undoubtedly be packed to the rafters to hear Mrs.

Sewall, lauded as a conquering heroine by her fellow suffragists. It was she who had first proposed an International Council of Women designed to seek the betterment of all humanity, including, but not exclusively, equal rights for women.[26]

As she walked, Anna reflected on Mrs. Sewall's strength of character. Earlier that day, Mrs. Sewall had talked with calm confidence of how her father raised her to believe "that woman was not better than man, nor man wiser than woman; that the government was not created by the good for the good, but the government was formed by the whole people, wise and foolish, good and bad; that there should be no taxation without representation."[27]

Anna had taken care to make her own speech just as forceful; strong enough, she hoped, to make even those old eternal doubters sit up and listen. It would also show Mrs. Sewall that Canadian women were every bit as committed to suffrage as their American sisters. As she entered the building, she stopped to discuss the final points of her strategy with her lieutenants, Dr. Eliza Ritchie and Mary Ritchie. Dr. Angwin was not present, but together the three women were Anna's best and boldest allies in the local fight for suffrage. Like Anna, these women had gone boldly forth to pursue careers regardless of the dangers and objections.[28]

Anna looked straight ahead, at no one in particular, as the master of ceremonies introduced her with gushing praise: "She is an enthusiastic advocate—indeed, the leader—of the movement for the enfranchisement of women: and is one of the most active and most eloquent members of the Woman's National Council."[29] Taking a deep breath, Anna came straight to the point, a habit she had acquired when dealing with taciturn Thai officials, and now had no desire to break. "It is to be regretted that in Canada women are denied many of the privileges accorded to their sisters both in Europe and the United States, but the time is coming when we shall have our full share of work and responsibility."

At the time, it was nearly impossible for women to break out of their traditional molds of housewives and mothers. Only the largely unstimulating careers of teachers, midwives, nurses, servants or seamstresses were available to women, and then only to spinsters or widows. Husbands still had ultimate control over their wives' property. They could do what they liked with any goods or lands their wives might be lucky enough to own. Husbands were well within their rights to leave their wives penniless if they wished.

The women spectators in the gallery cheered Anna's defiant words, but she had just begun. Thanks to the shining example of Queen Victoria, she pointed out,

> women have not only proved their capacity for governing great nations, but have shewn wonderful capacity for affairs and proved herself to be a true helpmeet and co-worker, instead of a servant and plaything of a man![30]

Then Anna dropped her bombshell. Women, she said, should stop paying taxes altogether if they couldn't vote for or against what the money was spent on. How else could democracy be served? The female spectators were ecstatic; the *Morning Chronicle* remarked vaguely that "Mrs. Leonowens gave an excellent address, bristling with good points in favour of the extension of the franchise of the women of the land."[31]

Anna and her cohorts had been able to convert the Rev. Dr. Black to the suffragist cause as well, and he happily told the assembly he was "thoroughly convinced that woman should have a voice in municipal government, in educational matters." He was prepared to go even further: he hoped that the time was coming when women would sit side by side with men in the legislative halls, having an active part in the government of the land,[32] and was convinced anyone with a brain would agree with him. A surprising number of the male decision-makers did agree; many of the numerous provincial bills dealing with the suffrage question were defeated by a frustrating margin of only one or two votes.

Concerted efforts had begun in 1884, with an attempt to secure the right of unmarried women with property to vote in municipal elections and to sit on school boards. The motion was lost 12 to 11 when the speaker voted to break the tie; it was defeated again in 1886, but finally passed in 1887, minus the school board provision. Anna continued to agitate unsuccessfully for the right of unmarried women property owners to sit on school boards. Given her own strong opinions about education, it is not surprising that Anna would have fought so hard for the right of women to be able to help direct school policies and curriculae.

111

It was a fight she continued to lead right up until she left the city in 1897. Her arguments and those of like-minded colleagues met with only limited success. Women ratepayers had been granted the right to vote in school matters in 1881. In 1895, they became eligible to act as school trustees only in rural districts, and only where these positions were customarily elected.

Anna had been encouraged by the storm of suffrage activity in the 1890s. In the space of a decade, 34 separate petitions totalling 10,000 signatures had been put before the legislature, most of them from the Women's Christian Temperance Union. Between 1891 and 1897, six bills for provincial enfranchisement of women on the same basis as men (that is, whether or not they owned property) were introduced — but all were defeated.[33]

It had been a long, weary fight, but it was by no means over. The suffragist movement had existed for a century or more in one form or another. Mary Wollstonecraft had urged equal rights for women in the 18th century; John Stuart Mill was among the most influential to take up the cry in the 19th. The demand for female equality had been spurred on by the anti-slavery feelings which ignited the American Civil War three decades before. Emancipation of slaves having been accomplished, the post-war sympathies of women turned to their own disenfranchisement.

In Nova Scotia, suffragists battled the indifference of other women as much as they did discrimination at the hands of men. In Halifax, the movement was never a populist one, except among women of outstanding accomplishment and intellectual ability like Anna, the misses Ritchie, Dr. Angwin and Mrs. Charles Archibald (then president of the WCTU and the Halifax Local Council of Women). Occasional rallies were often made by Mrs. Archibald's WCTU, which had agitated endlessly for prohibition since the Halifax chapter's formation in 1878 by an emissary of the crusading Frances Willard.

The WCTU's main preoccupation was to eradicate the sale and consumption of alcohol, perceived as the root of all evil. Its followers believed when women were given the vote, they would use their new power to demand prohibition legislation. Many women heeded the call to battle, and a provincial WCTU formed in 1881 to co-ordinate the many local chapters that had sprung up. But the war for Dominion suffrage and for temperance would not be won until 1918.

When the Women's Enfranchisement Association was formed in 1895 in Mrs. Charles Archibald's drawing room, its ambitions were to "awaken interest and qualify women to take a more active part...in all questions affecting their home duties, as well as in all public measures relative to their civic and state rights and obligation." The gauntlet had been thrown down, but less than two years later there would be no one to champion the cause. Despite the new group's membership in the Halifax Local Council of Women, it retained such a low profile that most people thought it had ceased to exist.

By 1897 and despite Anna's impassioned pleas, it might as well have. That year, only 282 property-owning single women voted in the municipal election out of 1,000 who were eligible, giving rise once again to the eternal speculation that sensible women just weren't interested in that sort of thing.

Anna, the Pianist, and Leipzig

Young Anna Fyshe burst into the morning room, breathless. "Madame Albani is coming! Have you heard?" Her grandmother had, as a matter of fact, heard. In fact, she had just heard it from Helen Kenny, sitting not two feet opposite, and stirring her tea with a smile as enigmatic as the Mona Lisa's. It was 1896, and Anna Fyshe was a student of piano at the Halifax Conservatory and a disciple of Mr. Charles Porter. Such was her talent that her grandmother had seen to it that she would continue her studies the following year in Leipzig, Germany.

Young Anna could barely contain her excitement at the news that Madame Albani, the internationally-renowned soprano, would be performing at the Halifax Academy of Music. Finally, Helen broke her uncharacteristically reserved silence. "I could introduce you to her if you like. I'll be seeing her on the 31st before the performance," she said, smiling sweetly. The teenaged Anna[34] was aghast. "We went to school together, Sacred Heart Convent in Montreal. She's from Quebec you know. Of course, in those days her name was Miss Lajeunesse."

The senior Anna smiled to herself at her friend's recollection. It wasn't the first time Helen's impeccable connections had earned her the astonishment of her social equals. In 1882, she had impulsively invited the dark and dashing 28-year-old Oscar Wilde to dinner. He had been in Halifax giving one of his popular lectures at Orpheus Hall, and he quickly accepted the invitation.

113

No doubt he was keen to meet the woman as renowned for her beauty as for her skills as a hostess. Helen, who took part in virtually every amateur theatrical production in town, would have been pleased to discuss drama, and partake of Mr. Wilde's famous Irish wit. For his part, Mr. Wilde was likely only too happy to discuss the success of his play, *Vera*, which had been produced that year in New York.[35] Neither was disappointed.

Anna, despite the enjoyment she derived from associating with the younger generation, belonged to a far different era. Her taste for theatricals was confined mostly to the tortuously long Ramayana, an epic Hindu legend taking 720 hours to perform. Yet there was more than an inkling of drama in her soul. Her own earlier books mixed intrigue, romance and exoticism, and would become one of Rodgers and Hammerstein's most successful musicals in the 1940s. Her grand-nephew, William Henry Pratt, left the stage for the silver screen, transfixing millions with his unusual Eurasian looks under the name Boris Karloff.[36]

Anna hoped her granddaughter would take to the concert stage. She was pleased at her namesake's burgeoning musical talent, already recognized throughout the city. Young Anna's scholastic and musical training had been immensely advanced by the founding of two new educational institutions in the city. Indeed, they shaped the direction of her life.

Reverend Laing, pastor of St. Matthew's just down the street, had been swept up in the fever of activity which surrounded Queen Victoria's Golden Jubilee celebrations in 1887. In a fit of monarchic zeal, he founded both the Halifax Ladies College and the Halifax Conservatory of Music. It seemed only natural that Mr. Porter, the church organist and choir master should become the Conservatory's first director. And since Anna saw him from time to time in church (she didn't hide the fact that she attended church sporadically, and then only for the music) it was only natural, too, that she should have a word with him about young Anna. None of the other children seemed interested in music. Young James was set on a medical career, and tiny Avis was showing a flair for drawing and painting. Max, thank God, had passed his supplemental high school exams after a dismal showing first time around.

It had been an embarrassing moment when Thomas Fyshe opened the morning paper to find his second son was not on the list of successful high school entrants. That the boy was only eight-and-a-half did not seem to matter to anyone. Anna quickly announced a summer of daily drills for Max, which James and young Anna were also compelled to attend. By fall, Grandmama had Max ship-shape for his first year of high school. He had just turned nine.[37]

Anna and Avis both attended Halifax Ladies College and were, typically, excellent students. They could scarcely have dared be anything else, with their reproachful grandmother just a block away down the street. Nor were they permitted to go to other children's houses to play, or even for parties. Perhaps, though, when Anna was out of town or otherwise occupied, their sweet-tempered but somewhat browbeaten mother would take pity on them and let them slip away for a picnic on the Northwest Arm, join a sleighing party, take the ferry across to Dartmouth for some fine lake skating, or stroll idly in Point Pleasant Park. If any of the young Fyshes ever experienced the sinful pleasure of a drive in a fashionable "Spider," a delicate two-seater carriage often used by city show-offs to court winsome young women, they would have wisely kept the secret knowledge to themselves.

By and large, life for the young members of the growing Fyshe family was an endless round of homework relieved only by fantastic tales à la Anna and there was always a moral to her stories.

A Farewell to Halifax

Whether Anna feared the corrupting influence of a Spider on her granddaughter, or whether it was simply fashionable, she had decided the young musician would finish her education abroad. Leipzig was a small but culturally significant German city where many of Halifax's musical instructors, including Mr. Porter, had studied.

If the younger Anna had any notions of independence, they were quickly quashed; Grandmama intended to accompany her protégé to Leipzig. The arrangement would work delightfully, at least from the senior Anna's perspective. She could keep an eye on the teenager who was already showing signs of rambunctiousness (Anna Fyshe still hadn't lived down a teacher's comment that she had become "noisy" in class) while attending University of Leipzig herself. Anna was particularly interested in a Sanskrit class the university offered.

Young Anna must have been a little relieved that her school chum Beatrice Whidden, a violinist, would also study in Germany that year, and perhaps provide some relief from her grandmother's constant attention.[38]

To Anna, the farewell to Halifax seemed as interminable as her departure from Thailand; for days, callers came to tell her how much they regretted her going. No one seemed to know how they would get along without her. The *Halifax Herald* was practically in mourning, but could not resist a swipe at others, who were not named, but obviously paled in her shadow: "So long dominated by a superficial and frivolous 'society,' Halifax cannot, without great loss, take a final farewell of Mrs. Leonowens."[39]

As Anna and company steamed off into the sunset that July day, the un-poetic epithet of the *Herald* reporter must have smarted a little in her ears:

What she has already done in Halifax will, like the concentric circles on the disturbed surface of a smooth lake, continue to expand till arrested by the distant shores.

Endnotes

1. Resolution of the Board of Directors of Victoria School of Art and Design, c. 1897, undated.

2. In 1925, VSAD became the Nova Scotia College of Art and Design (NSCAD), an internationally-renowned and progressive art school.

3. Anna lectured in Nova Scotia and Prince Edward Island on the need for formal art training through the establishment of such a school. She raised money as well as awareness through her lectures, and also had an American article called *The Art Movement in America* specially reprinted from *Century Magazine* which she circulated on behalf of the Victoria School of Art and Design in 1887.

4. *Halifax Morning Herald*. "Mrs. Leonowens' lecture," April 26, 1894, p.4.

5. *The Mercury*, Oct. 17, 1891.

6. French, Doris. *Ishbel and the Empire: A Biography of Lady Aberdeen*. Dundurn Press (Toronto and Oxford, 1988), p. 148.

7. *Halifax Herald*, June 19, 1897. In her book, Anna also pointed out, perhaps for good measure, that in Korea, Christianity was one of four national religions, and had been for many centuries. She took care, though, to mention that this had not been the result of the missionary influence. By then, she no longer felt that proselytizing people with an older, and very devout religious heritage was justifiable: it had backfired miserably on her missionary friends in Thailand, and they never won many converts.

8. Anna knew English, French, German, Guzerati, Hindustani, Thai, Malay, Arabic, Persian, Latin, Sanskrit and Pali, the latter two mostly found in specialized religious writings. She also learned some Russian for her trip to Moscow.

9. *New York Times*, Jan. 27, 1888, p. 8, col. 3.

10. This establishment still exists and has recently been restored to its former glory under the name The Waverley Inn.

11. Bank of Nova Scotia Archives, Fyshe letterbook. Letter to Mr. Mare, 28 March, 1888.

12. Bank of Nova Scotia Archives, Fyshe Letterbook. Fyshe to Mr. Greaves, 14 May, 1888.

13. Caroline Knox was the daughter of Sir Thomas George Knox, the British consul and Chau Phya Prang, a Thai princess. She and Louis were married in 1884. See W.S. Bristowe, *Louis and the King of Siam*. Chattow & Windus, 1976, p.86. This work contains a more thorough investigation of Louis's life.

14. Louis compensated for his loss with bouts of wildness. In 1895, so the legend goes, Louis rode his horse up the outside staircase of the Oriental Hotel (which he owned), burst unnanounced into the office of his manager, and sacked him. The manager claimed his accounts were eaten by white ants. In 1889, one of the Oriental's not-yet-famous guests was Joseph Conrad, then a ship's captain. The Oriental, these days considered the best hotel in the world, is so much a fixture of Bangkok that it is said its history is the history of Bangkok.

15. This was the exact word used by Jonathan Fyshe, of Edmonton, to describe his ancestor.

16. At the annual meeting of 1889, Anna's power to motivate was inadvertently paid tribute. It was noted that "the eloquent writings of Mrs. Leonowens and the grand success of the Worlds' Fair were thought to have awakened such a general interest in Art among our people as to make it desirable to engage an additional teacher and to open several new classes. It was soon found, however, that the enthusiasm which had been awakened had not much of the element of permanency." Whether this was a rebuke to Anna or an excuse for a lack of follow-through is not clear but it was evident the school was in trouble. Fine art classes, which had been a big money-maker, were thinly attended at best; only one pupil attended the etching class, and the deficit was running at $2,200.

17. Report of the second annual meeting of the Local Council of Halifax, in affiliation with the National Council of Women of Canada, March, 1896; report on Art Education in the Province and Report of the Art School, read by A. H. Leonowens.

18. Second annual meeting of the Halifax Local Council of Women, from a speech by Anna Leonowens.

19. *Ibid.*

20. The building, built in 1818, is now home to *The Five Fishermen Restaurant*, which has named a dish — Mushroom Caps Leonowens — in her honour. The college remained here until 1957; it moved twice more before settling at its present location in Halifax's Historic Properties. In a vintage building nearby is the appropriately-named Anna Leonowens Gallery, and just down the street is the new Art Gallery of Nova Scotia.

21. From a speech by Anna Leonowens before Lady Aberdeen at the inaugural meeting of the Halifax Local Council of Women, Aug. 25, 1894.

22. Nearly a century later, the United Nations would grapple with this problem and declare that all of humanity is entitled to decent housing, clothing, food, education and medical attention, a recognition of a primary, inalienable human right.

23. Other problems preoccupied the Council, too. It lobbied successfully for the appointment of a matron to the immigration sheds who could deal with the problems of newly-arrived women and children; it discussed what to do about unsuitable literature which was falling into the hands of students; and it developed a plan to reduce the long working hours demanded of women and children factory workers. In 1894, it founded the Home Teaching Society for the Blind, which began with a single instructor travelling the Maritimes teaching the blind to read.

24. *Evening Chronicle*, April 24, 1897.

25. Longley, J. W. Hon. in *Nova Scotia Debates*, 1893, p. 205.

26. Canada's National Council of Women did not adopt this platform until 1910.

27. *Morning Chronicle*, June 18, 1897.

28. Dr. Ritchie was the first female professor at Dalhousie College; Dr. Angwin was the city's first female physician.

29. *Halifax Herald*, June 19, 1897.

30. These remarks are taken from Anna's own notes, made at the first annual meeting of the Halifax Local Council of Women on December 13, 1894. She was the group's recording secretary.

31. *Morning Chronicle*, "Women want the franchise," June 18, 1897, p. 3, col. 1.

32. It was not until 1917 that women in cities and towns were extended the same rights, long after an unsuccessful attempt in 1910.

33. Cleverdon, Catharine Lyle, *The Woman Suffrage Movement in Canada*, University of Toronto Press (Toronto, 1950), pp. 157-9.

34. Anna Fyshe was then in her second year of high school at Halifax Ladies College, and would graduate in 1897 with a bronze governor-general's medal for general scholarship. She was born in 1881 or 1882, making her 15 or 16 years of age in 1896.

35. It is doubtful the Kenny's invitation would have been extended in 1895, despite the smashing success of his play, *The Importance of Being*

Earnest. It was the year of Wilde's disastrous trial and imprisonment for homosexuality. He wrote nothing more for the theatre, and died in 1900.

36. This interesting connection is outlined by Robin Duke in his introduction to a re-issued version of Anna's *English Governess at the Siamese Court.* Anna's niece, Eliza Sarah Millard married Edward Pratt, an Indian bureaucrat, and raised a family of eight sons and a daughter. William Henry Pratt worked at odd jobs in Canada for a while, but there is no evidence he knew about his famous great-aunt. His stage surname was allegedly the name of an ancestor.

37. Later, Max headed his own engineering and general contracting firm in Calgary.

38. Anna Harriet Leonowens Fyshe remarked that her grandmother never left her grandchildren alone "even for an hour." The overwhelming importance Anna and Thomas placed upon their education was stifling to the children; living up to their expectations was nearly impossible. (*Chatelaine, op.cit.*).

39. *Halifax Herald,* "Her Farewell to Halifax: Mrs. A. H. Leonowens' Influence Liberated a Million Siamese Slaves," June 14, 1897, p. 6, c. 1-2-3.

King Chulalongkorn at the height of his power as Supreme
King of Siam.

Chapter Five

Homeward Bound
1897-1915

"Oh, Mem, what have you done with your beautiful curls?" King Chulalongkorn held Anna tenderly by both arms and looked at her intently. "Well, Your Majesty," she replied, unfazed by his candour, "I just screwed them up on top of my head. Nowadays it is no longer the fashion to wear curls."

Anna met her favourite former pupil in London, England, on a warm day in August, 1897. It had been 30 years since they had last seen each other. He had grown into a handsome man, she thought, although he seemed a little pensive, burdened down, perhaps, by the awesome responsibilities that came with being an absolute monarch and venerated as a near living god in his own country. What she evidently didn't know was that he was already suffering the effects of a kidney disease, which would confine him periodically to a wheel chair, and cause his untimely death in 1910.[1]

Young Anna had remained as quiet as a mouse, hoping not to be noticed. But her grandmother was intent that the king take notice of the attractive young woman, and she pushed her gently forward for inspection. "Your Majesty, allow me to present my granddaughter, Anna Harriet Leonowens Fyshe. She is on her way to Leipzig to continue her studies in classical piano." The young Anna executed her best on-stage curtsy, but her face flamed red under the king's intense gaze.

They seated themselves on the divan, the early afternoon light poured in the window of the elegant London suite. Young Anna made no attempt to join in their tête-à-tête. She simply stared at the dapper, still handsome king dressed in elegant European clothes. She was barely able to contain her excitement, for he didn't look anything thing like she had imagined.

Chulalongkorn had ruled Thailand for 29 years. Under his leadership, the land had undergone significant changes. He had abolished slavery, and introduced automobiles just about the time they appeared in the United States. He had implemented a new system of government, making it accountable to parliament for the first time. Unfortunately, the measure was a miserable failure, except for the ministry run by his brother and right-hand man, Prince Devawongse. In what his officials considered a shocking departure from tradition, he built himself a homey, European-style villa of golden teak on the outskirts of the city overlooking a placid, man-made lake. He would often stay in a small guest house when the mood seized him to live like a commoner.

King Chulalongkorn had no wish to permanently escape the luxuries his vast wealth brought him, but he did not revel in it. Like his father, he was keenly interested in European culture, science and politics, and became the first Thai king to travel outside of his country. King Chulalongkorn was even proud to say that he had, in an entirely unheard-of move, appointed his wife, the Queen, to rule as Regent in his absence. Anna could only smile in approval.

His eagerness to see his children have a European education surpassed even that of his father's; eleven of his sons were currently studying at Eton and he could not restrain his enthusiasm as he showed Anna a photograph, taken only the week before, of the top hatted-and-tailed boys, arranged in ascending order, with the proud patriarch at the head of the line. But Chulalongkorn's aim was not simply to spend some of his ample funds on educating his sons. As he explained to an approving Anna, he wanted them to study useful professions like engineering, science and medicine so that when they returned home their skills would benefit their kingdom. It was customary for the numerous royal progeny to make up the bulk of the civil service; occupying powerful positions was their birthright. Chulalongkorn's notion that his sons should receive professional training in order to consciously benefit their country was another radical departure from tradition, fostered by Anna's early teaching.

Young Anna sat apart from her grandmother and the king, and fidgeted a little as they talked on and on. She had heard many of the stories before. Then there was a silence. She glanced over at the unlikely pair. The king was again looking intently at her grandmother. "Mem," he said finally, sadness creeping into his voice, "why did you write such a wicked book about my father King Mongkut? You know that you have made him utterly ridiculous and now the whole world laughs at your descriptions of him and at his memory. Oh, why, how could you do it?" Young Anna held her breath. How would her grandmother would answer?

The elder Anna had expected the king might refer to her book, but hadn't expected him to be so blunt. Anna had never been closer to having her carefully-created myth exploded, and she had no wish to be embarassed in front of her adoring grandchild. Anna knew she could hardly repudiate what she had written, for her books were now famous around the world. Surely King Chulalongkorn understood that she needed money and had taken the advice of her American friends on just what would make a good story. But she could hardly say that in front of her adoring granddaughter. Instinctively, she became defensive and, once again, overreacted in the presence of royalty:

> Your Majesty must surely understand that if I wrote a book at all about my life at the Court of Siam, I had to write the whole truth. And the truth is that your royal father King Mongkut was a ridiculous and cruel, wicked man.

Emotion coloured Anna's cheeks red. There was another long silence as the king stared at Anna in disbelief. Had Anna been alone with King Chulalongkorn, her response might have been different. But the king soon recovered himself, and resumed the conversation on another topic as if nothing had happened.

Young Anna Fyshe later recorded the incredible exchange in her journal, and her impression of the moment:

> Just like Grandmama, I thought, nothing ever stumps her....Finally the long talk came to an end. All seemed well once more and His Majesty was delighted with Grandmama's visit. We made our curtsies and parted as the best of friends.[2]

Grandmother and grandchild were quiet as they left the hotel following the interview. The senior Anna was unsure how to explain the incident to her grandchild. "You have just met a very brave man," Anna said finally. "Accomplishing what he set out to do has cost him more than any of us realize."

But the same was true for Anna, and her bones were weary. Anna wanted to devote her remaining energies to her

123

granddaughter, whose future looked so promising. They stayed three years in Leipzig, and young Anna's dedication and aptitude for piano performance and pedagogy made her grandmother proud.

As the century turned, Anna, by then nearly 70, returned to Canada, to make her home in yet another city. It would be her last home, for Anna's travels, but not her social crusading, were at an end.

Home Again

The seagulls had been following the ship all the way from Quebec City as it steamed down the mighty St. Lawrence. Anna marvelled at the neat seigneuries, laid out precisely so that each farm got a narrow share of valuable river-frontage. It reminded her of the Rhine River. Unconsciously, she began to hum *The Blue Danube* she sat wrapped in a blanket on the deck, having found a sunny spot just out of the chill wind.

She must have dozed a little, for when she opened her eyes, she was startled to see the outstretched arms of the Virgin Mary looming just above her from atop the reconstructed Notre Dame de Bonsecours cathedral. The ship was hardly moving, crawling past the Bonsecours Market building up to the quay. Montreal was so European she couldn't help but feel that perhaps she was not back in Canada at all. As they docked, she could see Avis and Thomas and all the children waiting for her. It was good to be home at last.

Later, over tea and raisin scones, she told the young people for the umpteenth time the story of King Chulalongkorn. They pestered her with questions all afternoon. Yes, he was very handsome indeed; he wore exquisite European suits, but no, she knew for a fact that he did not eat porridge for breakfast like they did. In fact, she told them it was a Thai custom to eat rice with spicy shredded meats and vegetables early in the morning. The children wrinkled their noses at the thought of such food, until she pointed out that lunch consisted of soup eaten with chopsticks. The children howled with laughter at what, to them, was a perfectly absurd notion.

They especially liked the story about the old Sanskrit teacher in Germany who first would not let her join his class because she was a woman, and who then tried to exclude her because he discovered she actually knew more of the language than he did.

"Why," someone exclaimed, "don't you go right over to McGill and offer them your services. You would make an excellent Sanskrit teacher, Grandmama."

Just then Avis came in and shooed them all away. She thought her mother looked weary after her voyage, or perhaps it was just age. As they went together up the stairs of the rambling, elegantly-appointed house, Anna stopped on the landing and gazed out across the McGill campus. An odd-looking, temple-like building on the corner had caught her eye. She asked Avis what it was. "Dilcoosha," Avis answered. The name meant "Heart's Delight" in Hindustani. Anna nodded in approval.

Charity Begins at Home

Already, a season had passed. Anna looked up towards Mount Royal, past the hulk of Ravenscrag, the mansion built by Sir Montagu Allen, then the richest man in Canada. How lovely the woods look; Montreal in winter was a little like St. Petersburg. Surely, Anna thought, only the Russian capital could match the elegant sleighs and prancing horses which paraded along Sherbrooke Street, bells tinkling. She loved to watch as every Saturday afternoon dozens of sleighs wound in a procession up the mountain.

Tobogganing, too, was popular and aficionados would glide down McTavish Street itself on snowy days. But the real challenge was up on Mount Royal where special runs nearly 180 feet high were constructed each season. Toboggans would hurtle down at nearly 70 miles per hour, an unthinkable speed. Now and then, the Fyshes would make the drive up the mountain; Anna always shivered a little in the sharp air, marvelling at the air-borne ski-jumpers, the snowshoers, the tobagonners, and the hockey players and curlers at Victoria Rink, all of them insensible to the cold.[3]

But Anna did not restrict her life to the ivory tower of her elegant Montreal neighbourhood. She had always cared for the poor, particularly women and children, and their suffering profoundly disturbed her. Even in Montreal, no Bombay or Calcutta by any stretch of the imagination, there was misery all around her. Once again, she rolled up her sleeves and waded into the fray, attempting to put right some of the disorder.

Griffintown, named for an Irish soap maker who first settled there, was considered an embarassment by its more well-to-do neighbours up the hill who wished it would simply go away. But its 40,000 inhabitants would not simply disappear overnight, despite the sickness and disease which raged through its grey industrial streets, encouraged by the scandalously unsanitary conditions. Griffintown's streets flooded regularly; diphtheria and typhoid were common, as they were in Halifax. Not surprisingly, Griffintowners died twice as fast as residents of Montreal's upper-class neighbourhoods.

Anna focussed her attention on the Baby and Foundling Hospital, and again, perhaps unconsciously, found herself walking in the footsteps of Lady (now Countess) Aberdeen. The Governor-General's wife had been distressed by the practice of baby farming which she learned about during a visit to that same foundling hospital some years earlier. Orphan babies were left in the care of foster families, who were given a lump sum payment to look after them. Often, the babies died mysteriously and the families pocketed the money. "There is no registration of births necessary in this province at all," the Countess railed,

> [...] the influence of the priests keeps up a very strong feeling about illegitimate children and the consequence is that it is accepted as a belief that the kindest thing is to baptize these children and then facilitate their exit from the world...the babies are farmed out with the result that...the percentage of deaths some years has been as high as 90 p.c & one year actually 99 percent.[4]

The Roman Catholic clergy were, perhaps, by now, more familiar with Anna than the Presbyterians for she had taken exception not only to baby farming, but to the common practice of hurrying newborn infants to church for baptism. The priests, no doubt, had no choice but to listen as she set out her reasons, that exposure to the cold air caused pneumonia and other potential ailments. Her arguments apparently had some effect.[5]

It was a Sunday morning. Anna listened to the pealing of the church bells all around her, but did not hasten to get ready for church. She had many to choose from, for, as Mark Twain had once observed on a visit, Montreal was a city in which one could not throw a brick without breaking a church window. Nominally Presbyterian (the household, including servants, ostensibly followed the religion of its patriarch), she was also a student of Buddhism and of Hinduism. For Anna, it was easy to see the essential truths of life in all three religions. "I am too good a Christian not to be something of a Buddhist, and too good a Buddhist not to be something of a Christian,"[6] she often said.

By 1860, Montreal had grown into the 10th ranked city in North America, boasting paved streets with gas lamps and a population of nearly 100,000. That same year, as Hugh Allen's workmen were labouring up at Ravenscrag, the Victoria Bridge was completed. The biggest in the world, the bridge took 3,000 men 10 years to build. Finally, Montreal was linked with the south shore of the St. Lawrence and American trade routes. Montreal's boom continued for many years afterwards.

The philanthropy of those same merchant princes (who controlled much of Montreal's commerce) was essential for the construction and upkeep of the city's many benevolent institutions. Among them was Peter Redpath, who gave half his fortune to McGill University, and the Redpath Library and Redpath Museum were testimony to his generosity.[7]

Anna often spent hours in the great reading room of the Redpath Library, just across the street from her home.[8] Armed armed with several books from the library's voluminous Chinese collection, she like nothing better than to sit in front of the library's gigantic fireplace and sift through them. Anna continued to lecture and write despite the early warning signs of advancing age.

After only a year in Montreal, she was already a popular lecturer. She was to speak that evening on Egyptian antiquities. Anna had written the original draft when she was only 16, while on an extensive tour of the Middle East with Reverend Badger. Even after reviewing the Egyptian collection at the Redpath Museum, she was pleased that only minor changes to the manuscript had been necessary.

Avis was especially looking forward to her mother's lecture. But first, they were expected at a five to seven o'clock musical which was to feature popular local performers. For the peckish, there would also be petits fours to nibble and cream tea to sip. Avis adjusted her petticoats under her long, silk skirt as she stood before the looking glass. A tightly cinched corset made her waist seem smaller than it was, even after six children. It was by no means a flashy dress, but most certainly stylish and very much in the expensive, understated style of her social set. Earlier in the day, Avis's long hair had been done up elaborately by a skillful maid; the enormous hat that she wore added several inches of height.

Avis had always marvelled at her mother's talents, and her ability to penetrate into any circle she decided to be a part of. It had taken almost no time at all for Anna to find a way into the circle of McGill academics. Anna could hold her own in any philosophical or religious discussion; politics also roused her debating instincts. The combination of Anna and her exotic tales enlivened many a gathering and threatened to upstage altogether that somewhat pompous professor of political science, Stephen Leacock, with his tweed jackets and his folksy, understated humour.

Avis was completely lost in her own thoughts when Thomas, in his best evening dress, came into her dressing room. It was nearly five o'clock; they would be late for the musical and the lecture both if they didn't hurry, he told his wife as he peered over her shoulder to adjust his cravat and smooth his hair. Penetrating eyes gave him a certain aura of power; his glance was not deceiving, for Thomas Fyshe had become one of the country's most prominent and successful bankers.

After final glances in the mirror, the elegant couple descended the staircase together, received their cloaks from the maid, and stepped out the front door in the fading evening light and into their waiting carriage, ready to whisk them down Sherbrooke Street through the swirling snow.

Anna's lecture that evening was a resounding success. But all of Anna's worldly successes would seem hollow a few short months later, when Avis suddenly died of food poisoning while on a trip to Toronto with Thomas. Anna had not borne the death of her dear daughter with her usual stoicism. It was such a silly, senseless accident, and Anna couldn't help but think that James, who was studying medicine right here in Montreal, might have been able to help his mother.

Now, overwhelmed by grief, Anna stood at the window of the family conservatory, lost in thought and almost hidden by the fronds of a gigantic Boston fern. She couldn't help but feel that the fecund humidity and calming greenery were just like southeast Asia. Could she have left it so long ago?[9] She thought of that first parting with her daughter in Singapore when she had sent her to England for her schooling. How the little girl had cried over leaving. How Anna had worried for those six months when she had no word that Avis had reached British shores safely.

Just then, a hand touched her shoulder. It was young Anna. "Grandmama, it's time." Time to bury another loved one as she had buried her husband, her mother, and her two little babies. She sighed, and a tear escaped from the corner of her eye. She leaned heavily on Anna's arm as she walked to the vestibule. The maid handed her a new pair of black gloves, and Avis helped her put on the broad-brimmed black hat with its long, black veil. She stood at the door for a few minutes, unwilling to go out into the bright sunlight until Thomas took her arm and helped her into the waiting carriage.

As the funeral cortège wound up the steep Côte des Neiges road that sunny afternoon two days past May Day, twisting around Mount Royal Park towards the cemetery, Anna, lost in her grief, hoped her dear Avis was safe once again. But Anna could hardly hope for rest now. She was thrust into the role of mother to a boisterous household of eight children, and comfort to her grieving son-in-law.

The untimely death of her cherished daughter had been a blow, but Anna had stepped in with her customary businesslike manner, and taken over the household. She did not allow the cook to do the shopping, but insisted on taking over that chore herself, accompanied by young Kathleen Fyshe or sometimes Louis's daughter, Anna Harriet, who never went anywhere without her dastardly long, thin dog. Anna often scolded Anna Harriet when she would go out into the street, whistling like a mad fiend after the animal, which escaped at every opportunity.

Anna's scolding was all to no avail. The darkly beautiful Anna Harriet would just laugh, a quicksilver laugh like her father. Her grandmother would smile, indulging for once a granddaughter's high spirits.

Anna continued to campaign vigorously for better health and social conditions for the less fortunate, but perhaps a little less vigorously than in the past; the fire of life was beginning to leave her. But she was well satisfied with the accomplishments of her grandchildren. James, his brother Max, sisters Anna, Avis and cousin Anna Harriet attended McGill University between 1901 and 1913, routinely bringing home medals and prizes. James enrolled in the Harvard arts program, but by 1901 had switched to McGill, earning a bachelor of arts degree. By 1904, he had graduated from the honours medical program, standing seventh in his class. Upon graduation, James had been hired by the Montreal General Hospital as resident physician, then had moved to the Alexandra Hospital for Contagious Diseases as medical superintendent. The next year, he sailed east.

First and Favourite?

> ... in going to Siam Dr. Fyshe is taking service under the king, whose knowledge of European civilization and customs was obtained from Mrs. Leonowens, Dr. Fyshe's grandmother, who was appointed to Bangkok by the foreign office as governess of the royal family of Siam when the present king was a child of five.
>
> *Halifax Morning Chronicle*
> September 27, 1907.

James, now Dr. J. C. Fyshe, had just given up a prominent position at Montreal's Alexandra Hospital for Contagious Diseases and headed off for an adventure. Anna was pleased, but just a little sad to see him go. It was James who she had sat on her knee even before he was old enough to understand, as she regaled him with stories of Thailand, of Buddhism, of right and wrong, and most of all, of the importance of rendering assistance to those less fortunate. It had its effect, for this favourite grandchild soon followed in his grandmother's adventurous footsteps.

The 29-year-old, green-eyed, brown-haired James was to become assistant medical officer of health and superintendent of the Government Hospital in Bangkok, Thailand. Four months later, he was received on the quay with all the pomp Uncle Louis (by then a trusted adviser of the king, and an accomplished adventurer in his own right) could muster.

Uncle Louis had re-married in 1899 at the age of 43. His 20-year-old bride, Reta May Maclaughlan, was closer in age to her husband's son and daughter! Their first visit to Canada had been in 1904. Reta stayed on over the winter with the Fyshes, getting to know her mother-in-law better, while Louis went to England to oversee the incorporation of the Louis Thomas Leonowens Co.[10]

For the newly-arrived nephew, overseeing hygiene for all eight million inhabitants of Thailand proved a daunting task. Scientific explanations were rarely ascribed to diseases, and the wheels of Thai bureaucracy, including the health department, turned painstakingly slowly. Sometimes they did not turn at all.

Malaria, cholera, dysentery, typhoid and smallpox raged, making it a land where men and women rarely lived past middle age. This explained Louis's preoccupation with parties (he was known to travel up-country with his own troupe of boxers, acrobats and dancers for amusement) and the good life in general.

But James didn't fall for the good life quite the same way that his Uncle Louis had. His thoughts were not on the Thai beauties; James was in love with a Montreal girl, Julia Corisande Mattice, nicknamed Zulu.

James was 30 when they were married, in an elegant ceremony in Bangkok. The new Mrs. Fyshe, by all accounts delighted with her new and exotic life, wrote gushingly to her grandmother-in-law about the fine reception, and again about an extravagant English-style Christmas dinner party complete with roast turkey, plum pudding and champagne — all served in the heart of the sweltering Orient.[11] Louis's Bangkok couldn't have been more different from the strict environment Anna cultivated for her grandchildren at home, and James soon lost his taste for life in the Orient.

By the time his son Thomas turned two James felt strongly that the child should be raised in Canada. The deciding factor may have been James's declining opinion of the Siamese health system, and he was every bit as opinionated as his grandmother. Seeing he could do nothing, he resigned his position. Perhaps his grandmother would have preferred he stay and do his utmost to be a catalyst for change, as she had been. In any event, he quickly sailed for home.

James returned to Montreal to become the General Hospital's first general superintendent;[12] no doubt he enlivened 70 McTavish Street as Louis had done before him with his Siamese stories. Uncle Louis' shoes were large ones to fill. During his 1910 visit, he created a sensation amongst the impressionable young fry. For his daughter's coming out party he sent dresses not only for Anna Harriet, but for Avis and Kathleen, too.[13] But the happy times were coming to an end for all of them. On James's homeward voyage he had received news his father had died on November 26, 1911.

Thomas Fyshe had retired from high finance in 1907. But his repose was shortlived: Prime Minister Sir Wilfred Laurier called on him to sit as one of three commissioners on a Royal Commission into the federal civil service. The commission issued a report which was hailed as a "a landmark in the reform of the Canadian civil service," and which shaped the modern bureaucracy which exists today.[14]

But in 1909 tragedy struck. Thomas had put himself under intense pressure as he laboured to produce the report. Shortly after completing the project, he collapsed with a stroke. Who was left to nurse him but his devoted mother-in-law? She kept him alive through sheer willpower long after doctors had given up hope. For his three remaining years he was completely paralyzed. On November 27, 1911, he had a second, fatal stroke. He was 66.

The *Montreal Star* and the *Montreal Gazette* carried long tributes to his banking ability, his long record of public service and his intense personality. Although Anna had never once complained about having devoted herself to her invalid son-in-law at the expense of her own speaking engagements, her writing, and her many charitable causes, the omission of her name was evidence that the formidable Mrs. Leonowens had been, after only three years, forgotten by the press.

Yet Anna had continued her informal lectures on Sanskrit at McGill until the age of 78.[15] She just could not bring herself to give up teaching. In every pupil, she saw a potential King Chulalongkorn or Lady Son Klin, but no one, not even her own grandchildren ever took her teachings quite so much to heart again. Out of all the grandchildren, only Anna Fyshe, her young namesake, had followed in her grandmother's footsteps and become a teacher.

Anna, in her rapidly-advancing old age, took comfort in her beloved Rig Veda, the great Hindu epic of which she never tired. She still read and translated its verses from the Sanskrit every day. Only rarely, did she peruse the fragile manuscript with the great poem written on palm leaves, which she had obtained in Bangkok. Like its owner, the pages were crumbled and dry with age.

But Anna's life contained one more triumph.

Meeting Mr. Kipling

> What did the Colonel's Lady think?
> Nobody never knew.
> Somebody asked the Sergeant's Wife,
> An' she told 'em true!
>
> —"The Ladies" by Rudyard Kipling[16]

The neighbourhood was buzzing. Rudyard Kipling, that year's Nobel Prize winner for literature was coming to speak. His appearance promised to be one of the big events of the season, for he was said to be a gifted orator. It was 1907, and a fine autumn day, Anna thought, as she adjusted her bonnet, put on a new pair of gloves, and set off to meet Mr. Kipling.

Anna had received a special invitation to meet the Nobel laureate; she looked forward to the occasion with an anticipation she had not felt since meeting the Beecher family. Although the paths of Anna Leonowens and Rudyard Kipling had never crossed, their lives, and views, were parallel in many ways. Kipling had been born in India, and separated from his parents at a young age to attend school in England. He returned to India at age 17. Shortly after, he began working on various newspapers and publishing volumes of poetry and prose; his artistic bent came naturally, for his father was a teacher of sculpture at the Bombay School of Art.

In 1889, Kipling left India to conquer the world. But the world wasn't quite ready for him. The New York publishers who had welcomed Anna's exotic tales were openly hostile to his. In London, the reaction was cool indifference.

Like Anna, Mr. Kipling was fascinated by Indian life; one of his favourite themes was the psychological and moral problems of the English "living in the midst of a subject people." Much of his work mirrored Anna's own firm views on the immorality of the British subjection of India. (Anna refused to refer to herself as British, and always said "the British" instead.)

Mr. Kipling's writing did not celebrate the Empire but rather the life of the private soldier. His sagas were often couched in language considered rather picturesque for the time, and for that, he won a fan in Anna, who must have smiled secretly at his linguistic liberties.

It soon became apparent that Mr. Kipling had abandoned his former brashness. During his cross-Canada tour, he professed a willingness espouse whatever opinion the majority of his audience held. To those who wanted to exclude Asians from settling in Canada, he declared,

> The time is coming when you will have to choose between the desired reinforcements of your own stock and blood and the undesired of races to whom you are strangers, whose speech you do not understand and from

whose instincts and traditions you are separated by thousands of years.

To Ottawa politicians, who had hoped to ignore the burgeoning racial problems on the west coast, he said:

I do not understand how the Dominion proposes to control the enormous Oriental trade and at the same time hold herself aloof from the Asiatic influx which is the natural concomitant of that trade.[17]

Not surprisingly, Mr. Kipling "received in Canada such a welcome as would scarcely have been given to any other private individual of his generation."[18] But the hypocrisy of the Nobel laureate's words did not go unnoticed. *Saturday Night* noticed the discrepancy and did not hesitate to state that it found Mr. Kipling most unoriginal.

Anna had noticed the wavering, too (in Thailand, such behaviour earned wafflers the unbecoming nickname, "weather-vane"). But she could not deny that Kipling was immensely popular with his audiences. She knew well enough that people did not necessarily want to hear the truth. She could have told the Nobel laureate a thing or two about growing up as the child of a British soldier in India, but she chose otherwise. Not only would the rather unsavoury details of her own life have destroyed the impact of all of his poems (the ribald "The Ladies," included), but she would have destroyed herself, too. Victorians were decidedly queasy about social climbers like her.

Having sent the coachman home with an empty carriage, Anna walked slowly along Dorchester Street. She turned in through the gate of the Grey Nun's convent, and sat for a moment on the little stone bench just inside. She had been on her guard with Mr. Kipling, particularly when the discussion had turned to army life in India. If her secret got out, she would be denounced as a fake despite her accomplishments. And that Mr. Kipling had a habit of ferreting things out of people.

Anna realized she had not thought about her childhood for some time. She had left that part of herself behind many decades and many continents ago. Like a snake that had shed its skin, Anna had shed all vestiges of her early life. She was comfortable in the life she had created.

With a shock, Anna realized that there was no longer anyone living who knew the whole truth about her background; not even

Louis had ever known. How could she ever tell anyone now of all the tricks of fate that had changed her life so utterly? But why should she? It hardly mattered now. What did matter was that she had made her own way in the world. Surely she had the right to make her own history as well. She had no regrets.

Anna rose from the bench, no longer relishing the prospect of the long walk back to McTavish Street. She stopped for a moment to admire Mount Royal looming ahead of her. No one, she decided, would ever know the true story.

The Death of Anna

The front door banged shut. "Avis, is that you?" called a muffled, slightly querulous voice from above. "Yes, Grandmama!" Avis put down her parcels and took off her wrap and hat before hurrying up to her grandmother's darkened sitting room. The old woman sat on the sofa, staring straight ahead. She turned her head toward the sound of Avis' footsteps. "What time is it Avis?" "Half past six, Grandmama," she said, putting on the light beside her. "I'll get your tea."

Anna Leonowens nodded to her grandchild, but continued to sit stiffly on the sofa. A few moments later, Avis bustled back with the tray. Pouring a cup, Avis cooled it for a moment on a saucer. There were good days and bad days. Today, Avis thought, as she watched her grandmother sip absently from the cup, she wasn't so bad. Some days, holding a teacup on her own was impossible for Anna, and Avis would have to spoon the hot drink into her like a child. "Careful, Grandmama, you'll spill it," she cautioned, taking the cup from her. "Oh Avis," sighed the old woman. "It seems you are no longer my granddaughter and my pupil; you have become a sister and a mother to me."

Anna had never forgotten any of her old pupils, especially little Fa-Ying whose talent for drawing had been so captivating that she had for once relaxed her usual emphasis on scholarship. Avis Fyshe, her grandmother's near-constant companion in her old age, was by then an accomplished calligrapher, artist and illustrator. She had become well-known for her Christmas card designs. Perhaps she was even more talented than the royal Fa-Ying, but by then, Anna could no longer read her fine calligraphy or appreciate any of her William Blake-inspired drawings. The formidable Anna was formidable no more.

It was 1914, nearly three years since Anna had suffered the stroke that blinded her, and she drifted in and out of lucidity. Lately, though, Anna had taken more and more to her bed, dreaming, young Avis supposed, of the Orient. The household had still been grieving over the death of the patriarch when Anna's own health broke down. Coping with Thomas's death and the strain of caring for the remaining Fyshe children had been too much for her elderly body; she, too, suffered a stroke. To make matters worse, Anna had never told anyone that she was actually three years older than she had always maintained.

Poor young Avis, who had always been her grandmother's helper, had virtually taken charge of the household. Kathleen, George and Anna Harriet were still at home. Anna Harriet was studying hard in McGill's English program. Anna Fyshe had continued her musical career, and was living in Germany after having married a Berliner. Max, too, had married and was operating a successful engineering firm in Westmount.[19] World War I had broken out in Europe, and James and Frank had been sent to the front.[20]

Young Avis had been a little sad the day Grandmama had said she would no longer host her Monday afternoon at-homes, but that had not stopped a successive round of callers, young and old, who constantly came to enquire after her health. When she felt up to it, Grandmama would have one or two guests in. They would ask her about former times, like her epic verbal battles with King Mongkut, or the days and nights she spent riding alone on the Trans-Siberian Express. Anna was always pleased to not only answer their questions, but to regale them for hours with the scenes that still flashed so vividly before her.

But even so close to death, Anna hadn't quite relinquished her hold on the day-to-day affairs of the household. Her grandchildren sat with her daily to tell in detail what they had seen, done and heard (particularly the latest news from James and Frank). They had watched their grandmother sink slowly into graceful old age after a lifetime of adventure. She had regularly held open houses for their friends, fellow McGill students who flocked from the campus across the road to hear her ever-entertaining tales, and to debate eastern philosophy and religion.

"Avis! Avis!" Her grandmother's sharp voice roused the girl from her reverie.

"What is it Grandmama? What's the matter?"

"I'd like a story, Avis. Read to me please."

Obligingly, Avis went to the bookshelf to select a volume. "What would you like, Grandmama?" she asked, taking down a book of myths and legends she was sure would please the old lady. "How about 'The Sorrow of Demeter?'" Anna nodded. Avis settled back and began to read:

> Now Persephone was with her she returned to the neglected earth, and the grain sprouted and came up green in the fields, and leaves crowded out on the trees, and the meadows and glades were thick with flowers. In due time came harvest, and the tall, ripe corn was cut and bound into sheaves; there was abundance as of old, because the grief and anger of Demeter were at an end.[21]

Avis looked up and saw that her grandmother had fallen asleep. Gently, she pulled the bright comforter around the thin shoulders, and tiptoed out.

It was just after New Year's, 1915, and Anna had taken to her bed for good. She was 84. As she lay in her upstairs room in the chill January evening, she tried to focus her mind of Buddha's teachings. Her lips moved slightly as she repeated the words to herself: "There is no self, nothing belongs to a self." The thoughts tumbled faster now, leaping one over top the other as she recalled the words of the old Thai monk who had been her language teacher, who had first explained the fundamental precepts of the Buddhist afterlife to her:

> There is a sphere which is neither earth, nor water, nor fire, nor air, which is not the sphere of the infinity of space, nor the sphere of the infinity of consciousness, the sphere of nothingness, the sphere of neither perception nor non-perception, which is neither this world nor the other world, neither sun nor moon. I deny that it is coming or going, enduring, death or birth. It is only the end of suffering.[22]

At that moment, she knew she would not live to see another spring. She tried to remember all the springs she had known, but they had melded into one endless garden stretching away into the distance. She could see only flowers, flowers and more flowers.

Anna died January 19, 1915. Two days later, at 2 p.m., the bells tolled in Christ Church Cathedral for her. The funeral procession wound down Saint Catherine Street, and up the hill to Mount Royal Cemetery where she was buried near her daughter and son-in-law. A Celtic cross marks the grave, which lies on the sunny side of Rose Hill. Below it is carved the inscription,

> Duty was the guide of her life
> and the love of her heart.
> To her, life was beautiful and good.
> She was a benediction to all who knew her,
> a branch of the spirit of God.[23]

News of Anna's demise was carried in the *Montreal Star* and *Montreal Gazette* the next day; it did not reach Halifax until January 23, when the *Halifax Herald* reprinted the Montreal obituary under the headline, "Death in Montreal of a former Halifax Lady:"

> Mrs. A. H. Leonowens died yesterday at her late [sic] residence, 70 McTavish Street, in her eighty-first year. The late Mrs. Leonowens, who came to the city with the family of her son-in-law, the late Thomas Fyshe, in 1897, formed many close friendships and was untiring in her efforts in charitable, religious and philanthropic work. She had a special interest in the Baby and Foundling Hospital of which she was president for some years, and notably assisted in the work to provide the present comfortable home for that institution. Some short time ago she suffered a stroke of paralysis thru which she had to curtail her activities. The widow of Major Leonowens of the British India Service, she was shortly after her husband's death selected to fill the position of governess to the late King of Siam. So satisfactory were her duties performed that the King later called on her in London to thank her personally for her work, and the care that had been bestowed upon him.... The late Mrs. Leonowens is survived by her son, Major Leonowens.[24]

In death, as in life, the legend remained intact; Anna's secret self was never revealed.

Endnotes

1. It has been suggested, but not supported, that Chulalongkorn did not have kidney disease at all but had succumbed to drug addiction and the delights of the harem, and was gradually removing himself from his formerly heavy involvement in running the Thai government.

2. *Chatelaine, op.cit.*, p. 62.

3. Fortunately, many of these have been preserved through some 400,000 negatives taken by the Notman studios in Canada over 50 years.

4. Gwynn, Sandra. *The Private Capital*, McClelland & Stewart, (Toronto, 1984; rpt. 1985), p. 278.

5. Collard, Edgar Andrew. "When Anna came to Canada," in the *Montreal Gazette*, Jan. 27, 1979.

6. *Ibid.*

7. Peter Redpath died in 1894 in England, where he had retired 15 years earlier.

8. Kathleen Fyshe, youngest daughter of Avis and Thomas, married Ronald Redpath.

9. The Fyshe house was on the edge of what would later become known as The Square Mile, the area of town inhabited exclusively by Montreal's merchant princes. There was greenery everywhere — lawns, orchards and gardens, and, in the days before southern winter holidays, nearly every house was equipped with its own "conservatory" or greenhouse.

10. Bristowe, *op.cit*, p. 99. Louis died in England in the post-war 'flu epidemic. When Reta died in 1936, she left the bulk of her considerable estate to Thai charities, including money for the building of the Chulalongkorn Hospital. No doubt Anna would have been pleased.

11. Bristow, *op.cit*, p. 126.

12. The restless and highly principled James was soon on the move, turning up soon after at Edmonton's newly-founded Royal Alexandra Hospital. During his stay there, he helped found the Alberta Hospital Association, and later became the hospital's administrator.

13. Bristowe, *op.cit*, p. 128.

14. *The Scotiabank Story, op.cit.*, p. 83.

15. While the Fyshe family believed Anna lectured at McGill, there is no actual record of this. For several years, the McGill academic calendar shows a blank in place of the name of one of its two Sanskrit instructors. McGill archivists have suggested Anna may have been the other instructor, that she may have lectured on a part-time basis or that she may have given informal tutorials.

16. Abrams, Donaldson, Smith et al, eds. *Rudyard Kipling's Verse, Definitive Edition*, "The Ladies," Bantam Doubleday Dell Publishing Group Inc.

17. *Saturday Night*, vol. 21, October 26, 1907, p. 1.

18. *Ibid.*

19. Max graduated with a honours Bachelor of Science degree in civil engineering, winning the British Association Medal and Prize, and took Honours in designing, geodesy and the theory of structures. That year, *Old McGill* annual saw fit to put beside his name an inscription which suggests a still-favourite student pastime: "For he by geometric scale/Could take the size of pots of ale."

20. James left with the Canadian Expeditionary Force from Quebec City on Sept. 19, 1914. He was soon Europe-bound as medical officer with the Fourth Battalion. Later appointed senior medical officer with the First Canadian Infantry, he was promoted to Major and earned several medals. Frank was killed in action.

21. Smith, Evelyn. "The Sorrow of Demeter" in *Myths & Legends of Many Lands*, vol. 1, Thomas Nelson and Sons Ltd. (London, 1930; rpt. 1947), p. 31.

22. *Bechert, Heinz and Richard Gombrich, eds. The World of Buddhism*, Facts on File Publications (New York, 1984), p. 23.

23. In 1983, the grave was inexplicably desecrated by vandals. A new and much sturdier monument has since been erected, marking the graves of her grandchildren Avis and Max, and Max's wife, Olivia Primrose Bayne.

24. *Halifax Herald*, Jan. 23, 1915, p. 7.

Anna Leonowens in old age: "…a face whose complexion had been ruined by the climate of the Orient." Notman photograph of a painting by Robert Harris, now in the possession of Anna's great-grandson, Dr Thomas Fyshe, Hamilton, Ont.

Epilogue

Aspirations and Aspersions

Sadly, [...] she destroyed her credibility as a historian by embroidering an intrinsically fascinating tale with unnecessary and inaccurate additions. Her reasons for this were purely commercial — now, as before, she was merely trying to earn her living, and generous helpings of skulduggery and scandal have always done wonders for book sales. [1]

Julia Keay

Anna's non-comformist ways, her lack of reserve and tact, her lack of belief in the wrath of God, and her insistence on associating with all classes and types of people, continues to make her enemies long after her death. Yet she could dazzle those she really wanted to impress with her keen intelligence, her frankness, and her repartee.

Anna's loquaciousness did not stop her from being tight-fisted, for she was positively money-grubbing, and constantly worried about her finances despite her impressive salary. People around her, Buddhist and Christian alike, showed nowhere near the same concern for their earthly well-being.

Anna didn't even bother to attend church regularly, but seemed to prefer whiling away her free hours in local temples attending various ceremonies, conversing with the local people in their own languages, and absorbing their culture.

Her sense of justice, which she held even as a child, is all the more remarkable for being out of step with the thinking of the time. As a 16-year-old girl, Anna was present at a dinner discussion of British supremacy in India. The guests agreed that the natives had to be put in their place from time to time. At that time, Anna did not have the courage to voice her unspoken thought, "And what is their place in their own country?" She was rarely silent again on any issue that touched her as deeply.

Yet it was hard to wreak any change upon the ancient and established order of social hierarchy, which did not easily admit the bold, the enthusiastic, the bright or even the newly successful into its upper folds. Anna's newfound desire to eliminate the petty class prejudices which forever shackled people to their backgrounds was not just a product of her own frustrations. It was echoed, in various forms, in popular literature of the time, by writers like Victor Hugo, Charles Dickens, Thomas Hardy and George Eliot. Although not everyone wanted to see the class barriers come down, commitments to various good works to better the lives of the common people was a popular pastime of the upper class.

Anna wanted to communicate her reformist sympathies to the world, but she also needed to make some money. Not long after her Siamese sojourn, an irresistible opportunity to do both presented itself. Assisted by her own fertile imagination, she would write her memoirs.

Anna quickly set to work and produced a heroine whose delicate body hid a fiery personality. She sensed, rightly, that a true-life account of her own worldliness, her complex opinions, feelings and rough-and-ready experiences would not cause Victorian readers to rush to their booksellers to buy copies.

What would intrigue readers were the very incidents she had experienced, told through the eyes of a naive and apparently helplessness young widow.[2]

King Mongkut's death in 1868 cleared the way for publication of the quasi-autobiographical series of articles which became her first book, *The English Governess at the Siamese Court*. These days, sophisticated readers can easily discern and discard the exaggerations which, for nineteenth century readers, only added to the drama of the story. Her influence over the king was undoubtedly inflated, and her missions of mercy throughout the streets of Bangkok may have been something less than the crusading life-and-death struggles she related.

It does appear Anna had reached a point in her life when she wished to be treated like the lady she felt she had become. She demanded, and eventually received, respect, despite King Mongkut's erratic and rather daunting wielding of his absolute power. She withstood not only his constant demands on her time, but the occasional attempt to intimidate her into submission, so that she would be more like the women around her.[3] Certainly Anna was not the only expatriate living in Bangkok to have found the King to be capricious in the extreme. Many

Americans and Britons could corroborate her stories with tales of their own.

Yet for all the wealth and power at his fingertips, the king was temperate in his habits, and an attentive, even indulgent father who respected his children's independence; nor was he a stranger to humility. King Mongkut had led the "homeless life" of a monk for nearly three decades, begging for his food every morning, forbidden to touch money or women, or even to engage in idle chatter. Instead, he devoted his time to study and meditation, and, after rising to the rank of abbot, led a reform movement which imposed stricter rules on monks.

Another of her claims, this one of fundamental importance to the story, has gone undetected. A key point in both *The English Governess* and *Siamese Harem Life* was her tutoring of the Crown Prince of Thailand. While she did instruct the young Chulalongkorn for a period of time, and obviously had a great influence on him, the boy had never been intended as his father's successor nor, as she indicated, was he being groomed (in part by her) for that post at the time of her Siamese sojourn.

It is no wonder, having shown such finesse in managing her own career, that the legend of the White Angel of Bangkok not only survived the death of its originator but grew larger than life.

Anna's posthumous fame was cultivated by overblown tributes to her wisdom, fortitude, resilience and tenderness. An evidently smitten John McNaughton, a McGill professor, heartily lamented his friend's death in a lengthy and moving tribute, describing her, even in great-grandmotherhood, as "one of the fairest sights in the flower-garden of English womanhood" who suffered unspeakable cruelties at the hands of a man he described as "His Omnipotence the Ogre."[4]

Anna's fame was also based, in no small measure, on a certain inherent racism that evolved from her heroic act of putting the infidel King of Siam in his place. While Anna never made such a claim (this is part of the legend which grew up around her), the attitude and the actions remain celebrated in later re-creations. The less dramatic side of Anna Leonowens life, and the one of intrinsically greater value, has been all but forgotten.

Knowing the full story only makes her attitudes about freedom and equal rights, her commitment to pacifism, to social welfare, to religious tolerance, to education, the arts and feminism so much more interesting. Her revulsion for class and caste, her unquestioning acceptance of religious freedoms, her delight in new cultures, languages and customs, and her fearless denunciation of what she thought unjust make her a true heroine.

Notably, Canada was the only place Anna ever really settled down. Although the presence of her family was the primary reason for her adoption of this country as her own, she also found in Canada a climate where her dauntless spirit, her boundless intelligence and her desire to see equality for all citizens could flourish. Anna was also a first-class adventurer, travelling alone across entire continents, suffering the hardships of jungle and steppe without complaint.

But her overriding concern was for her family, to whom her sense of devotion was intense. For them, she willingly sacrificed personal opportunities, changed her plans and, indeed, her whole life. But she never sacrificed her unending desire to see more, to do more, to learn more, and, in the process, to make the world a slightly better place.

Although her English governess persona continues to shine, the things which made the *real* Anna unusual, and a pioneer in her own time have been forgotten. It is a sad commentary, underscoring not only the shortness of our collective memories, but the obscurity of the role of women in general (perhaps this is because relatively few women are venerated as heroines, even fewer Canadians).

Anna's dreams launched her on an eight-decade journey through the wonders of the world. Fittingly, it was Canada she finally called home.

Endnotes

1. Keay, Julia. *With Passport and Parasol*, BBC Books (London, 1989), p. 50.
2. It does not seem to have crossed anyone's mind that Anna might have consciously intended to create a work of fiction. Certainly, the "novel" genre had been long established by writers like Daniel Defoe, although his wildly popular *Robinson Crusoe* (1719) and *Moll Flanders* (1722) were purportedly true stories. (The first real "novels," i.e., works of fiction put forth as such, came in 1740 and 1743, respectively, with the publication of Samuel Richardson's *Pamela*, and Henry Fielding's *Joseph Andrews*.
3. Once, she was even attacked physically by thugs who she suspected of being directed by members of the Royal Court, although she knew they were likely not directed by the king. Her Persian teacher, Moonshee, was also attacked and soon left the country.
4. MacNaughton, John, "Mrs. Leonowens," orig. published in *The University Magazine* (McGill University, 1915; rpt. *Essays and Addresses*), pp. 286-311.

Appendix A

Anna's Homes

Halifax

Although it is somewhat less so now, a certain devilry of spirit that would have been all too evident in Anna's time remains in present-day Halifax. It is particularly evident, just as it would have been 100 years ago, along Argyle, Grafton, Barrington, Market, Prince and George Streets on any given Saturday night. In the mid- to late-1800s, these streets — particularly Albermarle and North Barrack (now known as Market and Brunswick streets, respectively) — were the sites of countless taverns and brothels catering to the soldiers in the barracks of the Citadel above.

Anna and the Fyshe family lived in numerous houses that must have kept the family packing and unpacking every few years during its 19-year tenure in the city.[1]

All but one of Anna's homes are still standing. Many of the homes of her friends and acquaintances can also be found, along with most of the public buildings she spoke in. The few plaques marking their locations do not mention Anna, but through the osmosis of lore and legend that prevails in Halifax, the remains of Anna's life there can still be found.

The Halifax directory for 1876/77 shows Thomas Fish [sic], listed as an accountant, boarding at 106 Morris street (next to the former Morris St. Public School). Fyshe would have brought his bride (and, of course, his mother-in-law) to the family's first home, Hillside Cottage, in 1878. The cottage, owned by Henry Pryor and located off Jubilee Road overlooking the Northwest Arm, burned down sometime after August, 1938.

The family didn't tarry long at Hillside Cottage; the 1878-79 directory shows them living at 48 Inglis Street (now 5480 Inglis, at the corner of South Bland Street), part of a terrace of three town houses recently restored as condominiums called Bishop's Row. Not far away was Thorndean, the residence of J.S. MacLean (at the time, the Bank of Nova Scotia president and Thomas Fyshe's boss), where Anna promptly inaugurated a Shakespeare Club to encourage reading of the classics.

The family remained at 48 Inglis St. for a comparatively long time, not moving until 1883. That year they removed to Sunnyside, near the Northwest Arm, to a cottage owned by Andrew Kerr MacKinley, owner of a stationer's, printing firm and bookstore on Granville Street.[2]

There the family stayed until 1888, when Anna and Avis took the children abroad for their education, chiefly in Germany. During this time, a lonely Thomas Fyshe apparently lodged first at the bank (this may or may not have been the case: the city directory lists it as his home address), and later, in 1890-91, at 190 Hollis Street, in a building next door to, and owned by, the bank. From 1892 to 1894, he boarded at Waverley House, on Pleasant Street (now The Waverley Inn, at 1264-1266 Barrington), a famous inn run by the Misses Rowans.[3]

Montreal

In 1897, the expanding Fyshe family set up house in Montreal. In 1898-1899, they are listed in Lovell's Montreal Directory as living at 211 Drummond Street at Sherbrooke, and Thomas Fyshe as manager of the Merchant's Bank of Canada on 205 St. James St. Nearby, at 209 Drummond, lived Mrs. E. M. Greenshields, a widow of the insurance agent, along with Oswald J. Greenshields, a stockbroker. At 241 lived F. L. Wanklyn, manager of the Montreal Street Railway Co.

The following year, they moved to 70 McTavish Street, where they remained for 20 years. It was a convenient location, with the McGill College Library just across the street, in the shadow of the Montreal Water High Level Pumping Station (reservoir). That year, Thomas Fyshe was listed as general manager of the bank, in keeping with the family abode in the most elegant district of Montreal. Just up the hill, on the other side of the reservoir, was Ravenscrag, home of H. Montagu (Hugh) Allen, the richest man in Canada.

From 1912 to 1916, 70 McTavish's principal resident was apparently James Carlysle Fyshe, Superintendent of the Montreal General Hospital and later Capt. C.A.M.C., England. However, James was, in fact, in Alberta after 1913; he then enlisted in the army as a surgeon when World War I broke out. His brother, Frank, was killed in action. It would seem that the huge house at 70 McTavish was given up around 1916, for the 1917 city directories list no family members living there. Later, the house became a McGill University fraternity house. It has since been demolished and is now the site of the McGill Student Union building.

Endnotes

1. Certainly Anna must have always had her carpet-bag at the ready. She travelled frequently to New York and Boston, Britain and Europe, in between her literary, social, and organizational activities.
2. The house, at 3100 Dutch Village Road, adjacent to the Nova Scotia Teachers' Union building, is now owned by Piercey Investments Ltd. By car, the drive to downtown takes about 10 minutes; by horse and buggy, particularly in winter, the commute for Thomas Fyshe to the Bank of Nova Scotia on Hollis Street must have taken considerable time.
3. The Waverley had become, in recent times, a rather unsavoury hotel called the Sterling. It has since been renovated and re-named The Waverley Inn, hearkening back to its origins.

Appendix B

A Brief History of Thailand

Thailand's history encompasses numerous fiefdoms and cultures, including that of the Khmers, the Mons (who imported Buddhism from India) and the Thai people themselves, who were likely driven southward by Kublai Khan's militaristic machinations in China in the twelfth century. Amongst its many capitals have been Chiang Rai, Chiang Mai, Ayuthaya, and finally Bangkok in 1782. In the eastern jungles, the Khmers built Angkor Wat thousands of years previously, but it was abandoned and the Khmers were pushed out of Thailand in the fifteenth century.[1]

British influence began in 1600; the East India Company was founded and a factory established at Ayuthaya sometime after 1612. The factory closed in 1684 and there was little official contact until nearly 1822, the British having settled on the Island of Penang, Malaysia in 1791. In 1821, they sent John Crawford to Bangkok to attract some Thai attention to the new colony but because of his deep ignorance of local customs, he failed miserably. He was less than enamoured of Bangkok, writing that year that

> The few streets that Bangkok boasted, were passable on foot only in dry weather; the principal shops, however, and the most valuable merchandise were found along the river

in the floating houses, occupied almost exclusively by Chinese.[2]

In the nineteenth century, when the French, Dutch and British were busy colonizing the rest of south-east Asia, Thailand remained independent. King Mongkut (also known as Rama IV) and King Chulalongkorn (Rama V) are credited with "deftly playing one European power off against another."[3] At the same time, because of the willingness of these two kings to modernize the country, many of the benefits of colonialism were obtained, without its yoke.

King Mongkut distrusted the French and wanted to encourage British trade while holding onto all his fractious tributary provinces. He did not manage to accomplish this, losing the eastern jungle provinces (consisting, in part, of Cochin China and what would become French Indo-China, including parts of what are today Cambodia and Vietnam) to the French. Yet Thailand proper was never dominated by French, British or Dutch.

In 1824, the British conquered Lower Burma and it was feared that an ancient prediction that a foreign king would conquer Siam would hold true. That year, King Mongkut's brother, Rama III, usurped his more legitimate claim to the throne; Mongkut became a Buddhist priest, and remained so for the next 27 years, learning English, Latin, and Pali (the sacred language of Buddhism). Despite the isolation of his early life, upon ascending the throne he declared a sovereign should be accessible to his subjects. This view was part of a larger, enlightened philosophy resulted in his being hailed as Thailand's "first modern king."[4]

Trade treaties were signed with the British in 1822 and 1826 and with the U.S. in 1833, apparently to thwart threats from neighbouring countries. Later emissaries from the U.S. and Sir James Brooke, the English raja of Sarawak failed to produce trade agreements because, noted Virginia Thompson in 1941, there was no common language, and a decided ignorance of Siamese customs.

Endnotes

1. Anna was likely the first Western woman to see the massive complex, re-discovered in the 1860s by French explorer Henri Mouhot. Her masterful description lauded the impressive architecture and sheer

scope of the complex, in what is now Cambodia, and only within the past few years re-opened to tourists, although the area is still strewn with land mines, and is, therefore, extremely dangerous.

2. Jumsai, M. L. Manich. *King Mongkut and Sir John Bowring*, Chalermnit, Bangkok, 1970, p. 3.

3. Wheeler, Tony. *South-East Asia on a Shoestring*, Lonely Planet, Victoria, Australia, 1975; rpt. 1989, p. 566.

4. Thompson, Virginia. *Thailand: The New Siam*, The MacMillan Co., New York, p. 35.

Bibliography

Acadian Recorder. "The Review," June 22, 1887, p. 2., col. 4.

Akenson, Don. *At Face Value: The Life and Times of Eliza McCormack/John White*, McGill-Queen's University Press, Montreal & Kingston, 1990.

Angkrit, Phasa, ed. *Mongkut, King of Siam*, Bangkok, 1971.

"Art Movement in America, The," in *The Century Magazine*, The Century Co., New York; rpt. The Victoria School of Art and Design, Halifax, 1887.

Bank of Nova Scotia Archives, *Fyshe Letterbook. Fyshe to Mr. Greaves, 14 May, 1888; Fyshe to Mr. Mare, 28 March, 1888.*

Beaumont, Roger, *Sword of the Raj: The British Army in India, 1747-1947*, Bobbs-Merrill Co. Inc., Indianapolis, 1977.

Bechert, Heinz and Richard Gombrich, eds. *The World of Buddhism*, Facts on File Publications, New York, 1984.

Beecher Stowe, Harriet. *Uncle Tom's Cabin*, in *Readings from the Best Authors*, in the Nova Scotia School Series, A. & W. MacKinlay & Co., Halifax, 1865.

Berlingieri, Giorgio. *An Oriental Album: A collection of pictures and stories of an about the oldest hotel in Thailand*, D. K. Book House, Bangkok (undated).

Biddis, Michael. *The Age of the Masses*, Pelican Books, Middlesex, 1977.

Blake, Ruth. "Anna of Siam Lived in Canada," in *The Maritime Advocate and Busy East*, Jan. 1951, vol. 41, no. 6, pp. 9-12.

Blakeley, Phyllis R. "Anna of Siam in Canada," in *Atlantic Advocate*, Jan. 1967, vol. 57, no. 4, pp. 41-45.

Blakeley, Phyllis R. Notes and manuscripts from the Blakeley Collection, held at the Public Archives of Nova Scotia, including MG 1, vol. 3104, no. 1; vol. 3023; vol. 3025, nos. 14-26; vol. 3021, nos. 19 & 26; vol. 3092, no. 2; vol. 3093, nos. 18 & 19.

Bock, Carl S. *Temples and Elephants: The narrative of a journey of exploration through upper Siam and Lao*, Sampson Low, Marston, Searle & Rivington, London, 1884.

Bristowe, W. S. *Louis and the King of Siam*, Chatto & Windus, London, 1976.

Brown, Robert Craig and Ramsay Cook. *Canada 1896-1921: A Nation Transformed*, McClelland & Stewart, Toronto, 1974.

Bruce, Harry and Chic Harris. *A Basket of Apples: Recollections of Historic Nova Scotia*, Oxford University Press, Toronto, 1982.

Buckler, William E. ed. *Prose of the Victorian Period*, Houghton Mifflin Co., Boston, 1958.

Burns, H. D. "Thomas Fyshe, 1845-1911," in *Canadian Banker*, Autumn, 1951, pp. 77-83.

Cameron, Silver Donald. "From Siam to Halifax," in *Atlantic Insight*, Aug. 1988, pp. 18-20.

Chronicle Herald, "Granddaughter of novel's heroine dies," Nov. 7, 1961, p. 24.

Chronicle Herald, "Formidable Anna of Siam worked for women's rights in Canada," summer, 1990 (undated).

Churchill, Mrs. George. *Letters from My Home in India, Being the Correspondence of Mrs. George Churchill, 1871-1916*, ed. Mrs. Grace McLeod Rogers, McClelland, Goodchild & Stewart, Toronto, 1916.

Collard, Edgar Andrew. "When Anna came to Canada," in *Montreal Gazette*, Jan. 27, 1979.

____. "Anna in Montreal," in *Montreal Gazette*, Dec. 7, 1968.

____. "Montreal Yesterdays: More Stories from All Our Yesterdays", *The Gazette*, Montreal, 1989.

____. *Montreal: The Days That Are No More*, Doubleday, New York, 1976.

Collins, Lou. "City Streets are alive with tales of the past," in *Chronicle Herald* (undated).

Crowther, Geoff, Hugh Finlay et al. *India: A Travel Survival Kit*, Lonely Planet Publications, Victoira, Australia, 1981; rpt. 1991.

Cummings, Joe. *Thailand: A Travel Survival Kit*, Lonely Planet Publications, Fourth ed., Victoria, Australia, 1982; rpt. 1990.

Evening Chronicle "Ladies Musical Club decided to play bridge and had several grand slams," April 24, 1897. .

Evening Mail, "The Libraries of Halifax," Sept. 19, 1895, p. 4. cols. 1-3.

Farwell, Byron. *Burton: A Biography of Sir Richard Francis Burton*, Penguin Books, London, 1965; rpt. 1990.

Fingard, Judith. *The Dark Side of Life in Victorian Halifax*, Pottersfield Press, Halifax, 1989.

French Shackleton, Doris. *Ishbel and the Empire: A Biography of Lady Aberdeen*, Dundurn Press, Toronto, 1988.

Fyshe, Anna Harriet Leonowens. "Anna: From the Unpublished memoirs of Anna Harriet Leonowens Fyshe," in *Chatelaine*, Jan. 1962, pp. 60-64.

Gibbon, John Murray. *Our Old Montreal*, McClelland & Stewart, Toronto, 1947.

Gwynn, Sandra. *The Private Capital*, McClelland & Stewart, Toronto, 1984; rpt. 1985.

Halifax Herald, "Her Farewell to Halifax: Mrs. A. H. Leonowens' Influence Liberated a Million Siamese Slaves," June 14, 1897, p. 6, cols. 1-3.

Halifax Herald, "Mrs. Leonowens Tells a Thrilling Story of the Organization of the First Women's Council in India 2,000 Years Ago," Aug. 25, 1894, p. 5.

Halifax Ladies College, Record books held at the Public Archives of Nova Scotia, RG 14, series B.

Halifax Local Council of Women, Minute books, scrapbooks and annual reports held at the Public Archives of Nova Scotia, MG 20, vol. 1054, no. 4; MG 20, series 538, vol. 294-296.

Halifax Morning Herald, "Mrs. Leonowens' lecture," April 26, 1894, p. 4.

Hopkins, H. W. *City Atlas of Halifax, N.S., from Actual Surveys of Records*, Provincial Surveying and Pub. Co., Halifax, 1878.

International Council of Women. *Women in a Changing World: The dynamic story of the International Council of Women since 1888*, Routledge & Kegan Paul, London, 1966.

Jumsai, M. L. Manich. *King Mongkut and Sir John Bowring*, Chalermnit, Bangkok, 1970.

Keay, Julia. *With Passport and Parasol: The adventures of seven Victorian ladies*, BBC Books, London, 1988.

Landon, Margaret. *Anna and the King of Siam*, Harper and Row, New York, 1943.

Leonowens, Anna. *The English Governess at the Siamese Court*, Oxford University Press, Singapore, 1988.

Leonowens, Anna H. *The English Governess at the Siamese Court: Being recollections of six years in the royal palace at Bangkok*, intro. by Leigh Williams, Arthur Barker Ltd., London (rpt); orig. pub. 1870.

Leonowens, Anna H. *Siamese Harem Life*, intro. by Freya Stark, Arthur Barker Ltd., London (rpt); orig. pub. 1872 as *The Romance of the Harem*.

Leonowens, Anna H. *Life and Travel in India, Being recollections of a journey before the days of railroads*, Porter & Coates, Philadelphia, 1884.

Leonowens, Anna H. "Moscow, 'The Holy,'" in *The Critic*, June 1887, nos, 2,4 and 6; New York.

Leonowens, Anna H. "The English Governess at the Siamese Court," in *Atlantic Monthly*, Ed. James Freeman Clarke, published by Fields, Osgood and Co. April, 1870, vol. 25, pp. 396-410; May, 1870, pp. 554-565; June, 1870, p. 730; Aug., 1870, pp. 144-155; "The Favourite of the Harem," pp. 335-345 and "L'Ore, the Slave of a Siamese Queen," pp. 462-470, Sept. 1872.

Leonowens, Anna Harriet, Jr. "Across the Continent in a 'Flivver'" in *McGill News*, vol. iii, no. 4, Sept. 1922.

MacMillan, Cyrus. *McGill and Its Story, 1821-1921*, Oxford University Press, Toronto, 1921.

MacKay, D. C. "Heroine of 'Anna and the King of Siam' Among Founders of Art Institution," in *The Mail Star*, Dec. 6, 1968.

MacKay, Donald. *The Square Mile: Merchant Princes of Montreal*, Douglas & McIntyre, Vancouver/Toronto, 1987.

MacNaughton, Prof. John. "Mrs. Leonowens," in *The University Magazine*, McGill University, Montreal, 1915; rpt. *Essays and Addresses* (undated) pp. 287-311.

Mail-Star, "New Home for Leonowens Gallery," Jan. 21, 1975.

McGill News. Obituary of Dr. J. C. Fyshe, vol. iii, no. 4, Sept. 1922.

Mercury, The. Re: Mrs. J. F. (Helen) Kenny, Oct. 17, 1891, Halifax.

Mohout, Henri, *Travels in Siam, Cambodia and Laos, 1858-1860*, intro. by Michael Smithies, Oxford in Asia Hardback Reprints, Singapore, 1989.

Montreal Gazette, "Vandals desecrate grave of Anna (of Siam fame)," Oct. 20, 1983, p. A-6.

Morgan, J. W. *Canadian Men and Women of Our Time*, 1898 and 1912 editions, Toronto.

Morning Chronicle, "Women want the franchise," June 18, 1891, p. 1. cols 1-2.

New York Times, "Suit to recover grandfather's estate fradulently secured by C.P. & S. Dunn; Jury disagree, Jan. 24, p. 8, col. 3; Jan. 25, p. 8, col. 3; Jan. 26, p. 8, col. 1; Jan. 27, p. 3, col. 1; Jan. 28, p. 8. col. 3; Jan. 31., p. 8. col. 1; Feb. 1, p. 8. col. 3; Feb. 23, p. 8, col. 3; "Marriage of W. S. Paine," April 6, 1888, p. 4. col. 7; "Administrator C. F. Chickering sues for larger fee, Feb. 10, 1888, p. 8, col. 2; "Will Settled, J. H. Wardwell's claims disallowed," Jan. 1, 1888 p. 9, col. 7; "Executive suit to secure payment, Dec. 11, 1887, p. 8, col. 2.

Payzant, Joan M. *Halifax: Cornerstone of Canada*, Windsor Publications, Halifax, 1985.

Pearse, Harold. "Anna as Art Advocate and Educator," in *NSCAD Papers in Art Education '88*, Nova Scotia College of Art and Design, 1990.

Peck, Mary Biggar. *A Nova Scotia Album: Glimpses of the Way we Were*, Hounslow Press, Willowdale, 1989.

Raddall, Thomas. *Halifax, Warden of the North*, McClelland & Stewart, Toronto, 1948.

St. John Williams, Noel T. *Judy O'Grady and the Colonel's Lady: The Army Wife and Camp Follower Since 1660*, Brassey's Defense Publishers, London, 1988.

Saturday Night. "Kipling's visit to Canada," vol. 21, Oct. 26, 1907, p. 1; "Letters to the Family," vol. 21, May 16, 1908, p. 1.

Schull, Joseph, and James Douglas Gibson. *The Scotiabank Story*, MacMillan of Canada, Toronto, 1982.

Smith, Evelyn, ed. *Myths and Legends of Many Lands, vol. 1*, Thomas Nelson & Sons Ltd., London 1930; rpt. 1947.

Stacey, Robert and Liz Wylie. *Eighty/Twenty: 100 Years of the Nova Scotia College of Art and Design*, Art Gallery of Nova Scotia, Halifax, 1988.

Thompson, Virginia. *Thailand: The New Siam*, The MacMillan Co., New York, 1941.

Time. "New Musical in Manhattan," April 9, 1951.

Van Beek, Steve. *Bangkok, An Insight City Guide*, APA Publications, Singapore, 1988.

Victoria School of Art and Design. Minute and record books held at the Public Archives of Nova Scotia.

Williams, Leigh. *Green Prison*, Herbert Jenkins Ltd., London, 1943.